101 451 862 8

THE PAST IN PERSPECTIVE

Series Editors: C. C. Eldridge and Ralph A. Griffiths

D1341305

THE PAST IN PERSPECTIVE

Series Editors: C.C. Eldridge and Ralph A. Griffiths

C.C. Eldridge is Reader in History at St David's University College, Lampeter, University of Wales.

Ralph A. Griffiths is Professor of Medieval History at University College of Swansea, University of Wales.

Other titles in this series:

Revolution in Religion: The English Reformation, 1530–1570

David Loades

Protestant Dissenters in Wales, 1639–1689

Geraint H. Jenkins

Revolution in America: Britain and the Colonies, 1763–1776

Peter D.G. Thomas

The Road to 1789: From Reform to Revolution in France

Nora Temple

THE PAST IN PERSPECTIVE

IRELAND DIVIDED

THE ROOTS OF THE MODERN
IRISH PROBLEM

Michael Hughes

CARDIFF
UNIVERSITY OF WALES PRESS
1994

© Michael Hughes, 1994

British Library Cataloguing-In-Publication Data.
A catalogue record for this book is available from the British Library.

ISBN 0–7083–1243–8

Typeset by the Midlands Book Typesetting Company, Loughborough
Printed in Great Britain by Dinefwr Press, Llandybïe

For Mark

Contents

Editors' Foreword

Each volume in this series, *The Past in Perspective*, deals with a major theme of British, European or World history. The aim of the series is to engage the interest of all for whom knowledge of the riches of the world's historical experience is a delight, and in particular to meet the needs of students of history in universities and colleges – and at comparatively modest cost.

Each theme is tackled at sufficient length and in sufficient depth to allow each writer both to advance our understanding of the subject in the light of the most recent research, and to place his or her approach in due perspective. Accordingly, each volume contains a historiographical chapter which assesses how interpretations of its theme have developed, and have been criticized, endorsed, modified or discarded. Each volume, too, includes a section of substantial excerpts from key original sources: this reflects the importance of allowing the reader to come to his or her own conclusions about differing interpretations, and also the greater accessibility nowadays of original sources in print. Furthermore, in each volume there is a detailed bibliography which not only underpins the writer's own account and analysis, but also enables the reader to pursue the theme, or particular aspects of it, to even greater depth; the explosion of historical writing in the twentieth century makes such guidance invaluable. By these perspectives, taken together, each volume is an up-to-date, authoritative and substantial exploration of themes, ancient, medieval and modern, of British, European, American and World significance, after more than a century of the study and teaching of history.

C. C. Eldridge and Ralph A. Griffiths

Explanatory note
References to the Illustrative Documents which follow the main text are indicated by a bold roman numeral preceded by the word 'DOCUMENT', all within square brackets [**DOCUMENT XII**].

Preface

Mike Hughes died a premature, tragic death in 1993, while this book was in the press. Most of his career was spent teaching at the University College of Wales in Aberystwyth; in 1992 he moved to La Sainte Union College in Southampton.

He will be remembered chiefly as a distinguished historian of modern Germany. By the time of his death, he had numerous articles and four books to his credit, with other major works, including this one, in various stages of preparation. Peter Alter, Professor of Modern History at the University of Cologne, has written of the 'amazing breadth of interest' and the 'remarkable achievements' of this 'fair, understanding and critical scholar'.

His students remember an inspiring lecturer and a sensitive and understanding tutor. I remember the man. I remember him sitting in the sun on the holidays we all spent together, tightly laced into the shoes he polished every morning and buttoned into his tweed jacket, laughing his shoulder-shaking Santa Claus laugh and adjudicating on some wine or other. 'There we are' he says, and then he says it again.

Mike Hughes's studies of German history, particularly the rise of fascism, had engendered a deep-seated unease with forms of nationalism, 'a cloak for the self-seeking', as he was inclined to think. He deplored the use of myths to deceive or manipulate, and he applied common-sense and intellectual rigour to the analysis of motive. All forms of violence were anathema to him.

The relationship of Britain with her 'Celtic fringe' was something which fascinated him, and in *Ireland Divided* he brings his wide knowledge of European history to bear, focusing on the intertwining of myth and reality and on the interplay between integrity and self-deception. To Mike Hughes the pursuit of 'historical truth' was of the first importance.

Jane Cox
April 1994

Foreword

The bout of 'Troubles' which began in Northern Ireland in 1969 has lasted longer than any earlier outbreak. The Irish problem, the last and most stubbornly insoluble legacy of the British Empire, has levied a heavy toll in the lives of soldiers, policemen and other servants of the government and innocent bystanders. It has damaged Britain's international reputation and cost the British tax-payer enormous sums. This study sets out to explain the origins of the partition of Ireland, which is at the root of the problem. It arises from my interest in nationalism: I see the Northern Ireland problem as a clash of two nationalisms, claiming the same piece of soil as their own and sustained by powerful myths.

I acknowledge with gratitude permission to reproduce material in the documents section from the following: Times Newspapers Ltd. for Documents I, X and XI; the Bodleian Library, University of Oxford, for Document II; the National Museum of Ireland for Documents IV and VI; the National Library of Ireland for Document V; the Controller of Her Majesty's Stationery Office for Documents VIII and XVII; the Controller, Stationery Office, Dublin, for Document XV; Irish Academic Press for Documents XII and XVI reproduced from A. Mitchell and P. Ó Snodaigh (eds.), *Irish Political Documents, 1916–1949* (1985); the editor of the *Irish Independent* newspaper for Document XIV; the Master and Fellows of University College, Oxford, for Document XVIII. I am also very happy to record my thanks to the many people who have helped in one way or another during the production of this book: Mark, my son, and Yvonne, my wife, Professor and Mrs T. A. Watkins, Dr and Mrs J. E. Hoare, Dr and Mrs J. Marek, Dr and Mrs N. Cox, students in the History department at UCW Aberystwyth, the editors of the series, Ceinwen Jones and the staff of the University of Wales Press and the staffs of the Library at LSU College, Southampton, the Linenhall Library, Belfast, and the Library of the Queen's University, Belfast.

Michael Hughes

1.   Myth as History

There are in Northern Ireland two traditions or communities. Each has a mass following, each has a totally different vision of the past and of the future, and each claims the same piece of soil as its own. One group has gradually acquired the habits of deference and inferiority, the other the habits of command and superiority. The language, culture and religion of the one were long seen as better than those of the other. They are known by and call themselves a variety of different names; perhaps the most convenient are Unionists and Nationalists, which are more accurate than loyalists and republicans. Each claims to be part of a larger national group, British and Irish, though in reality they are now very different from these groups. Although the two have a great deal in common and both claim to be Irish, there is total misunderstanding between them and they see themselves as very different. Irish Nationalists, in both North and South, have often experienced difficulty when they seek to define 'Irishness', to lay down who is included in the Irish nation and who is excluded from it. This is nothing new: the concept of Irishness has been vague and shifting for centuries. In the period examined in this book those who have identified themselves simply as Irish and have claimed to speak for the Irish nation have found it particularly hard to accept the claim of Unionists, who are the descendants of only the latest of successive waves of migrants to Ireland, that they are at one and the same time Irish and British. Both of these unresolved problems remain at the heart of the Irish question today.

Obsession with history plays a major role in the formation of each group's image of itself. Over the centuries, both have been accumulating myths by which each defines itself and its position regarding the other. The Nationalists believe that they are the heirs of the original inhabitants of Northern Ireland, a distinct Irish nationality with its own language and culture, identifiable from the Iron Age until the middle years of the nineteenth century. Even after the decline of the Irish language as a consequence of the Great Famine of the 1840s, the

distinctiveness of this group did not disappear. The Roman Catholic
religion replaced language as the most obvious badge of Irishness. A
major element in the consciousness of this community has been a desire
to recreate the lost Ireland of the past, an idealized vision of Gaelic
Christian culture, something pure and uncontaminated, long protected
by the sea against the Romans, Dark Age barbarism and the horrors of
industrialization. In the twentieth century it was to be the ambition of
men like Éamon de Valera to re-create this lost world and to preserve
it as a society in aspic, a barrier against the godless materialism of the
modern age.

In the late sixteenth and early seventeenth centuries, the English
government carried out 'plantations' of Protestant settlers in the
north-east of Ireland as the first part of a comprehensive scheme
to solve what that government saw as the Irish 'problem'. Their
function was not merely to cement England's control of Ireland but
also to civilize the wild and dangerous native Irish. This reinforced
the long-established Scottish communities, especially in Antrim, whose
ancestors had settled there over the centuries. This very different
community became the forefathers of today's Unionists. These regard
themselves as custodians of an idealized vision of the 'British way of
life' and British liberty, symbolized by the Crown and the Union
between Britain and Northern Ireland, which they see as protecting
them against destruction by an alien Catholic Irish state.

For the Nationalist community, England's and Britain's involvement
in Ireland is an unending story of misrule, from which part of the island
escaped only with the establishment of an independent Irish state. Each
generation of Irishmen produced heroes who fought, and usually died,
to achieve this freedom. Time and again their efforts were betrayed by
compromisers, who tried to find an accommodation with the English.
The continuing British presence in Northern Ireland is the last relic
of this misrule.

For the Unionists, the English/British connection has brought nothing
but benefits to Ireland, enabling it to escape from its innate backwardness and tendency to anarchy. Throughout history violent and
self-seeking bigots have conspired to end the happy relationship in
order to feather their own nests. The Unionists see the end of the
Union as a certain disaster for the country.

The whole of Irish history could be satisfactorily squeezed into one
or other of these two versions. From the Middle Ages to Grattan's
parliament in 1782, the Irish parliament sought to defend Irish rights
against England's plan to turn the country into a colony; or, the Irish

parliament was a venal and ineffective bastion of privilege. From the outset the English government created an Anglicizing 'murder machine' to exterminate the Irish language and culture. Enough was preserved by clandestine 'hedge-schools', which also taught the Irish peasants Latin and Greek, to enable them to be revived successfully in the twentieth century. Conversely, Anglicization was part of a long-overdue modernization of Ireland, which a few sentimentalists tried to hold up by clinging to a dying language. Landlords who evicted tenants in the nineteenth century were rapacious absentees concerned only to milk the greatest profit from the land their ancestors had stolen from the people; or, landlords who evicted tenants were selfless agents of economic modernization who, by forcing people to emigrate, shook them out of their rural torpor and made available to them marvellous opportunities. The Black and Tans were devils incarnate, the sweepings of English prisons; or else they were the benevolent guardians of the innocent people of Ireland against a mafia of drunken gunmen out to loot and murder their way to power. And so on.

This situation has its roots in the historiography of Ireland as it developed in the nineteenth century, giving the stamp of scholarly legitimacy to many traditional myths. The Nationalist view was, for example, promoted by a revival of interest in Ireland's Celtic past in the early nineteenth century, of which, ironically, many of the originators were Anglo-Irish Protestants. The work of Gaelic enthusiasts on the Irish language and Irish antiquities was turned into evidence that the imposition of English rule had destroyed a free, orderly and highly cultured society. Examples were Alice Stopford Green's *The Making of Ireland and its Undoing* (1908) and *The Irish State to 1014* (1925). J. A. Froude's *The English in Ireland in the Eighteenth Century* (1872–4) presented an idyllic and completely inaccurate view of the benefits bestowed on the feckless and ungrateful Irish Catholics by the Protestant Ascendancy, based largely on a limited selection of records drawn up by the English administrators of Ireland in Dublin Castle. Froude portrayed the Ascendancy almost as pioneers, shouldering Kipling's white man's burden by ruling one of 'Your new-caught sullen peoples, Half devil and half child'. W. E. H. Lecky's *History of Ireland* (1892), an extract from his *History of England in the Eighteenth Century*, was designed as a refutation of Froude but was easily misinterpreted as a general attack on the Union. Such simplifications, purveyed through school books in Britain and Ireland, have not only affected the views of ordinary people. The ideas and attitudes of leading politicians in Britain and in the two Irish communities in the nineteenth and twentieth centuries were often formed by myths about Ireland's past. Policies which supposedly redressed past injustices acquired a moral as well as a utilitarian justification.

Historians began seriously to challenge this interpretation in the 1930s; they were led by T. W. Moody, whose pioneering work was to result in the Clarendon Press's multi-volume *New History of Ireland*. A new journal, *Irish Historical Studies*, has since 1938 been a standard-bearer of this revisionism. Its aim is to write objective unpartisan 'value-free history' without 'goodies' or 'baddies'. In articles in *Transactions of the Royal Historical Society*, 5th series, 33 (1983), 'History and the Irish question', and *History Today*, 34 (1984), 'The problems of writing Irish history', R. F. Foster describes the disputes caused by revisionism. Since the 1960s, with the opening of archives, the traditional interpretation has apparently been so completely demolished that in 1982 R. F. Foster could announce: 'We are all revisionists now.'

Foster was probably right, at least as far as the historical profession is concerned, though a few historians continue to fight a rearguard action in defence of some aspects of the old approach. Occasionally, also, a work appears which seems to have emerged, untouched by the new history, from a sealed time-capsule, for example, E. R. Norman's *Penguin History of Modern Ireland* (1971). There are brief statements of the two sides in the revisionist debate in 'Nationalist perspectives on the past: a symposium', in *Irish Review*, 4 (1988). In his attack on revisionism, Desmond Fennell, a self-confessed nationalist, argues that revisionist history is part of a general rejection by the new Irish élite of a republican tradition which has become an awkward barrier to the rapprochement with Britain which they seek for mutual benefit in the EEC and in Northern Ireland. He calls for a revival of 'the kind of history-writing and history-telling which sustains, energizes and bonds a nation and thus serves its wellbeing'. Other opponents of revisionism argue that the revisionists have gone too far in their efforts to eliminate bias, and accuse them of historicism and of engendering a view of the past as distorted as that which it seeks to replace. The revisionists have also been accused of having an ideological motivation, a desire to steal the Irish people's past by destroying the myths which are vital to their sense of national identity. Too often this national identity seems to be defined in narrowly Catholic and Gaelic terms. Jim Smyth, in his review of several new books on Irish history in the *Historical Journal* (1991), 'An entirely exceptional case: Ireland and the British problem', mocks some extreme examples of revisionism: those who died as a result of the Great Hunger of the 1840s were fortunate to be admitted to a life of bliss in the company of gentle Jesus earlier than might otherwise have been the case. R. V. Comerford, in his chapter on 'Post-famine Ireland' in volume 5 of *A New History of Ireland*, edited by W. E. Vaughan (1989), emphasized the continuing need for historians to challenge long-held myths, however valuable they might appear in forming an Irish national identity.

As a result, in part, of the revisionist controversy, students of Irish history now have available a magnificent range of works, from highly detailed monographs to sweeping syntheses, which make clear the deep complexity of the story. Unfortunately the old view of the past, which sees everything in simplistic terms as a conflict between Catholic and Protestant, English and Irish, Irish-speaker and English-speaker, has not been eliminated from the history taught in schools, and among the ordinary people of Ireland it retains a very tenacious hold. As always, what people believe happened is more important in forming their attitudes and influencing their behaviour than what professional historians demonstrate really happened. Revisionism has also had no effect whatsoever on the real politics of Northern Ireland or the Republic. All this contributes substantially to the intractability of the Irish question.

2.   The Roots of Partition

A factor central to the Irish problem and the fundamental cause of the partition of Ireland is the relationship between England (later Britain) and Ireland. English and British policies have played a major part in making Ireland what it is today. Foreign involvement in Ireland began with Viking settlements in the east, around Dublin, Wexford and Waterford. After the Norman Conquest the Roman Church in England claimed rights over the older Celtic Church in Ireland, which had survived after the departure of the Romans. Pope Gregory VII (1073–85) gave the see of Canterbury powers to carry through a reform of the Irish Church. In 1155 Adrian IV (the English pope) awarded overlordship of Ireland to King Henry II of England to enable him to carry out this reform. This award became the basis of the English Crown's claim to Ireland. English or Anglo-Norman influence was also invited into Ireland as a result of wars between individual rulers. The politically divided nature of the country and the absence of a unified Irish state were important factors in this process.

The impact of England was at first very limited. Irish culture remained remarkably vigorous and able to assimilate newcomers. English control over Ireland was very tenuous and the nominal overlordship claimed by the Crown was difficult to enforce. English political and cultural influences were long restricted to the area around Dublin, the Pale. Many Norman and other invaders up to the sixteenth century were quickly Gaelicized and came to see themselves as part of an Irish ruling class. Great Norman families like the Butlers and Fitzgeralds merged with the native aristocracy.

Real English control began to be exerted only in the late fifteenth century after Henry VII restored stability to England following the Wars of the Roses. The early Tudors used a dual approach, a combination of military force and a policy of divide and rule, exploiting the deep divisions within the Irish aristocracy. The Reformation in England was a major turning-point. It resulted in growing English nervousness that Continental enemies might use Ireland as a back door through which to attack England: there were Spanish landings in 1579, 1580 and 1601; later there were French landings.

In 1540 the Irish Parliament was summoned and in 1541 it was induced to declare Henry VIII king of Ireland. Nominally Ireland remained a separate state sharing the same monarch as England, but English policy intended to convert it into a colony of England. One method of achieving this was plantation, the clearing of the native Irish population from areas of land, which would then be resettled with reliable immigrants. The first attempted plantations were made under Edward VI on lands confiscated from rebels, but they failed, as did another attempt under Mary Tudor.

The first major plantations took place under Elizabeth I in 1584. Private contractors, known as undertakers, were given the job of recruiting settlers for half a million acres of land. In the event, very few could be induced to go to Ireland, which was regarded as a dangerous and uncivilized frontier region. Between 1595 and 1603 there was a great rising against the Crown in the north-eastern province of Ulster. This was eventually defeated, and the province was taken over by the Crown. Ironically, Ulster was traditionally the most rebellious and least pacified and the most Irish province in Ireland. The year 1607 saw the so-called flight of the earls, the exile of the native aristocracy. Ulster was then divided into counties on the English model in preparation for its resettlement.

In January 1609 the first comprehensive plantation scheme began. Twenty-three fortified new towns were set up, including Belfast, as a network of strong points to control the whole province. Recruitment of settlers was carried out by private undertakers, the London guilds and government agents. By 1622 some 21,000 English, Scottish and Welsh immigrants were in place. An Anglican aristocracy was installed, but a majority of the settlers were members of the Nonconformist Dissenter sects. They had to keep the native Irish as a labour force to work the land, but from the first the settlers were frightened of the people whose land they had stolen. They expressed this fear in mistrust and repression, and a siege mentality quickly grew up among them.

The situation became very complex in the period of the English civil wars. Royal agents engineered the so-called Great Rising, nominally in support of Charles I. During the rising a large number of Protestant Ulster planters were killed. They were to become part of the growing Protestant martyrology, so graphically illustrated in the gruesome pages of the perennially popular Foxe's *Book of Martyrs*. Bloody revenge for these atrocities was exacted during Oliver Cromwell's campaign in

Ireland in 1649. These victims of massacres and brutality were in their turn to become part of a growing Irish Catholic martyrology.

After 1649 it was the prime aim of the English government finally to solve the Irish 'problem' by means of further plantations. During the Commonwealth some 36,000 planters, many of them ex-soldiers, were given land. Again large-scale settlement was restricted to Ulster. Elsewhere the change mostly took the form of settlers becoming the ruling class and taking over ownership of the land while retaining the native Irish as labour. It is estimated that 80 per cent of the land in Munster and Leinster changed ownership. Resentment of this gigantic act of robbery fuelled Irish nationalism into the twentieth century. Only in Ulster was the settlement large enough to change the nature of society. Substantial emigration to Ulster, especially from Scotland, continued in the eighteenth century. It is from these people, not the original planters, that the majority of the present Ulster Protestants are descended. Outside Ulster only the top layer of society was changed with the imposition of an alien Anglican landlord class.

Further divisions between the settlers and the native Irish developed when King James II, after his deposition by William of Orange in the Glorious Revolution of 1688, landed in Ireland in March 1689 with a French army to try to recover his throne. In the course of James's invasion, another layer of myth was added. James, who offered a policy of religious toleration and concessions to Ireland, gathered much support from non-Anglican Protestants and Catholics, and his campaign quickly took on the character of a national Irish rising. Contrary to Unionist myth, Ulster did not at once throw in its lot with William III, as many regarded James as the legitimate king and there were religious divisions between Anglicans and Dissenters. In the case of the city of Londonderry, the magistrates were ready to open the gates to James but the initiative was seized by a small, radical Presbyterian group, the Apprentice Boys, who denied him entry, initiating a siege which was to become an important element in Unionist myth. The Battle of the Boyne on 1 July 1690, a date which was to become the holiest day in the Unionist calendar, saw the defeat of James. In the course of the repression which followed, some 120,000 Catholics went into exile, the so-called Wild Geese. This deprived the native Irish of their last leaders, and thereafter political, social and economic power in Ireland was in the hands of the Anglican Ascendancy.

The age of the Ascendancy, or of the penal laws, lasted from 1695 to 1829. During this period non-Anglicans were, in theory, not permitted to hold any offices, to vote, to be magistrates, to enter professions or to buy land. On the death of a Catholic, his or her lands were compulsorily divided among all children. There was no official Catholic education system. The Anglican Church was privileged, enjoying for example the right to take tithes from all, including non-Anglicans. Ireland remained nominally a separate kingdom with its own Parliament until the Act of Union in 1801, but the Parliament was dominated by a small group of Anglican nobles and gentry, the only people in Ireland with political rights, and it was easily manipulated by the London government. The same group also controlled local government in the Irish counties.

Much of this traditional view of the Ascendancy is pure myth, and the word itself is misleading. It would also be wrong to see all this as simply a product of bigotry or a blind clinging to power and privilege by a tiny élite. This was how Irish nationalism later portrayed it. Confessional states were typical of *ancien régime* Europe. Roman Catholics were viewed in Britain and Ireland as agents of a political system, popery and absolutism, rather than simply as a confessional group. Their refusal to conform in religion was seen as evidence that they must be enemies of the state. In practice, the penal laws were not strictly enforced, especially in the eighteenth century. The Catholic masses remained remarkably loyal to the Crown in spite of the repressive legislation. The late eighteenth century saw the growth of a small Catholic middle class of graziers and suppliers, and there were many conversions to Anglicanism. The Catholic Church remained apolitical, and there is no evidence of any widespread desire among Catholics to destroy the constitution.

Catholics were not the only targets of the penal laws. Non-Anglican Protestants were also unprivileged, and many Ulster Presbyterians became active in the revival of Irish nationalism in the late eighteenth century. Those long excluded from political power and people with progressive opinions began to organize to challenge the ruling clique. The influence of the American Revolution was considerable, and economic factors played a part. The main vehicle of the reform campaign was the Patriot movement led by Henry Grattan and Henry Flood. In 1779 this spawned the Volunteer movement, an armed force of 80,000 men. The government, unnerved by its defeat in the American colonies, was forced to make wide concessions to the reform movement in Ireland. The power of the small clique of aristocrats, which had run everything for over sixty years, was broken. The Irish Parliament was given wider legislative powers. There was growing pressure for a new constitution to establish a self-governing

Ireland, though some Protestants still had reservations about admitting Catholics to full political rights, especially because of fear of possible challenges to the great land transfers of earlier centuries.

In May 1782 a reforming government in England conceded a new Irish constitution, giving wider legislative powers to the Irish Parliament. As a result, Ireland became in theory a sovereign state sharing a common monarch with England. The picture was far from perfect: Catholics and Dissenters were still excluded from political power, and London was still able to manipulate the Irish Parliament through placemen. In spite of that, these reforms initiated a period of great optimism in Ireland, reflected in the construction in the 1780s of some of the finest public buildings in Dublin, including a new Parliament House (now the Bank of Ireland), the Customs House and the Four Courts, designed to show that the city was the capital of a real kingdom, not a colony. There was also growing prosperity in the mid-1780s, with high grain prices and rising linen and food exports. The economy was not, as later myth would have it, deliberately held back by the British government.

This optimism was misplaced. Before long an event took place which caused major changes in the constitutional relationship between Britain and Ireland, the so-called Great Rising of 1798. This was the culmination of a long period of mounting instability, caused largely by events outside Ireland, especially the French Revolution and the revolutionary wars. In that year a small group of revolutionary Irish nationalists tried to take advantage of Britain's involvement in war with the French to seize power.

The 1790s saw the rise of a new form of Irish nationalism, republicanism, strongly influenced by events in France and associated with the names of Wolfe Tone, Lord Edward Fitzgerald and James Napper Tandy. It was organized in the Society of United Irishmen in Belfast, established in 1791. It remained very much a minority movement but had centres of support in Dublin, Antrim and Down. It was radical and democratic. Although its membership was largely Protestant, it supported Catholic emancipation and abandoned the long-held belief that Catholics, because of their religion, were unfit for liberty. The long-assumed link between Catholicism and despotism was held to have been proved incorrect by recent events in France. Some leaders of the movement became involved in a conspiracy to mount a rising with French help.

There was a sharp reaction against the French in 1793 after the killing of the king, and a wave of loyalism swept Ireland. One manifestation of this was the foundation in 1794 of the Orange Order and the beginning of regular celebrations of the relief of Londonderry and the Battle of the Boyne. There was an outbreak of sectarian violence in Ulster, culminating in a minor religious civil war in County Armagh, as Protestantism again became equated with loyalism. Although this arose from competition for increasingly scarce land because of rapidly growing population levels, it was in the government's interests to politicize such religious divisions by promoting loyalism and Orangeism against the supposedly pro-French and treasonable Catholic United Irishmen.

The late 1790s saw an atmosphere of mounting crisis in Ireland, with attempted French landings and isolated insurrections. The government equipped itself with savage repressive powers, a Protestant yeomanry was set up, and attacks were launched against the United Irishmen in Ulster. The actual rising in 1798 was provoked by the brutality of the army, which used terrorist methods to stop an insurrection before it started. In southern Ireland it involved well-publicized atrocities against Protestants, answered with savage military repression. As so often, it quickly gave rise to a host of new myths and reinforced existing ones. The myth that it was a Catholic rising aimed at the extermination of the Protestants in Ireland quickly developed, and it effectively ended Protestant constitutional nationalism. It also produced the first clear signs of what was later to become Ulster Unionism; Ulster Nonconformists, who earlier were part of the anti-Ascendancy camp, began to make common cause with their Anglican fellow Protestants.

The rising convinced the government and sections of the ruling class in Ireland that only a full union between Britain and Ireland would remove forever the threat to Britain's security. Catholic leaders and the Catholic hierarchy were in favour of union because the British prime minister, Pitt, promised that it would lead to full Catholic emancipation. Ironically, many Anglicans opposed it out of fear that it would lead to concessions to the Catholics which would undermine their privileged position. The Irish Parliament, after some reservations, accepted the Act of Union, which came into effect on 1 January 1801. It involved the creation of a single Parliament for Britain and Ireland and the union of the Irish and English Anglican Churches. In the debates on the Union, speakers warned the Ascendancy that their position was usurped and threatened by the 'old inhabitants' of Ireland: only English military power sustained their position and the Union made no difference to this fact.

As was intended, the Union intensified the links between Ireland and Great Britain, which inevitably meant increasing domination of one by the other. Disillusionment was not long in coming. Pitt's promise of Catholic emancipation was not fulfilled because George III refused to agree to it. The end of the Napoleonic War in 1815 was followed by a slump, which hit Ireland hard and made the Union even more unpalatable. An Irish nationalism centred on Roman Catholicism soon appeared. In 1803 Robert Emmet, later regarded as a hero, organized a rising against the Union and was executed. Although this, and other similar insurrections, enjoyed little popular support, the Union was never accepted by the majority of Irish people and was always resented, not so much for itself but because it came to symbolize specific grievances. English rule came to be equated with religious repression, economic exploitation, cultural superiority and an alien ruling class. Dublin Castle, the seat of the administration, became the symbol of foreign rule.

The two forms of Irish nationalism which were to be dominant in the nineteenth century had their roots in the events of the 1790s. From the first, the most visible form of nationalism was constitutional, in that it aimed at persuading the English government to restore the sovereign Irish Parliament and Home Rule, which were supposed to have existed in the time of Grattan. Alongside this a conspiratorial, violent and revolutionary physical-force nationalism, which came to be known as Fenianism, was always present, though it usually involved very small numbers and was disapproved of by the Catholic Church and the majority of Irish people. Most 'Fenians' spent their time socializing rather than conspiring, but the myth was, as usual, more important than reality. This had its origins in another important Irish 'tradition' of the eighteenth century, resistance by secret societies. Groups like the Whiteboys and Rightboys in Munster and the Oakboys and Steelboys in Ulster went in for organized campaigns of rural terrorism. Initially these were not political but were more often anti-landlord or anti-tithe movements, but they established a tradition of resistance by conspiracy and violence.

The nationalist movement was always most successful when it was associated with a concrete issue or grievance rather than with Irish national independence as such – for example, Catholic rights, the long-standing land question, or the rights of Irish tenant farmers against their landlords. Rural discontent was perennial, and land agitations were frequent and violent throughout the nineteenth century. As a serious movement, Irish nationalism first emerged under Daniel

O'Connell, 'the Liberator' (1775–1847), a committed constitutionalist. His movement was closely allied to the Catholic Association of Ireland, which attracted a mass membership in support of Catholic emancipation. In 1829 a Catholic Relief Act removed the last disabilities, and from then on education, property and political influence were fully open to Catholics. This had the unfortunate effect of linking nationalism more closely to Catholicism. After the Famine of the 1840s, Catholicism and nationalism became even more intimately linked, as the Catholic faith became a substitute for the dying Gaelic culture. The Catholic clergy played a major role in O'Connell's movement, but the ambivalence of the Church towards nationalism remained. Its prime aim was to obtain religious concessions and to secure its own influence over the people. It was viciously hostile to the Fenians, who in turn attacked the clergy's interference in politics, while still remaining devout Catholics.

The developments of the late eighteenth and early nineteenth centuries also contributed to the consolidation of the other Irish community, the Unionists of the North. The enfranchisement of Catholics in 1829 provoked serious sectarian violence in Ulster. The 1820s saw a deep economic recession, which produced violence in many parts of Ireland. O'Connell and the Catholic emancipation movement and Protestant organizations both benefited from this.

The Great Hunger of 1845–9 also had a major impact on the development of nationalism. It completed the destruction of Gaelic culture. It also established the emigration tradition which led to a population decline shown in every census between 1851 and 1961. It built up a great reservoir of anti-British opinion among the Irish in the USA, Canada and Australia, which reinforced the Fenian movement. While only a tiny minority of property owners had the vote, constitutional nationalism had limited possibilities, and physical-force nationalism seemed to offer better prospects. An important physical-force organization, the Irish Republican Brotherhood, was established in 1858 in Dublin by James Stephens, John Devoy and Jeremiah O'Donovan Rossa. It had an estimated membership of 30,000 in Ireland, 10,000 in Britain and an unknown number in the USA, and planned to carry out a violent rising to establish an independent democratic Irish republic.

Oscar Wilde summed up the British approach to Ireland well: 'If in the last century England tried to govern Ireland with an insolence that was intensified by race hatred and religious prejudice, she has sought to rule her in this century with a stupidity that is aggravated by good intentions.' British governments swung between two methods of dealing with the Irish problem. One was concession: for example, support for Catholic education and state funding of the Catholic seminary at Maynooth. The other was coercion, which, though often short-term and employed with regret, reinforced resentment of British rule. The government was never able to treat Ireland as an integral part of the United Kingdom but always had to retain a substantial apparatus of repression there. An armed paramilitary 'national' police force, known after 1867 as the Royal Irish Constabulary, was established in 1836. Its members always served away from their home areas and lived in barracks. Habeas Corpus could be suspended, and a series of Coercion Acts – 105 were passed between 1800 and 1921 – gave the military wide powers. In Ireland there were severe restrictions on rights enjoyed in Britain.

British policy in Ireland was based on the belief that good government would eventually reconcile the Irish to English rule. This derived partly from gross ignorance of the situation in Ireland – it was said that British administrators knew more about Africa than Ireland – and partly from misplaced faith in the 'therapeutic' approach to problems, the belief that there is a remedy for all ills and, if one could go on trying long enough, one would be sure to find it eventually. This was a fundamental error. Although the majority of Irish people were not against the maintenance of a link with Britain, they wanted Home Rule, seeing it as the only answer to Irish problems.

During the 1870s and 1880s two important developments took place: the Irish question became one of the most important issues in British politics, and Irish nationalism revived as a mass movement with various manifestations, including an organized nationalist parliamentary party and a new cultural nationalist movement. These two developments were linked, and shared some common causes.

Certain political changes during the period had very important consequences. Measures of electoral reform, carried through in 1868, 1872 and 1884–5, brought in the secret ballot and considerably enlarged the electorate. The last of these created universal adult male suffrage and revolutionized politics in Ireland. There was also much greater literacy in the country. One result of these changes was the rise in the 1870s of the Irish Parliamentary Party (IPP), which grew out of the Home Rule League founded in 1873 under Isaac Butt. It aimed to use its weight at Westminster to win Home Rule by constitutional methods. The first time it put up candidates, in the 1874 election, it won fifty-six seats. This marked the collapse of what has been described as deference politics, the system on which the great landlords' political power was based. The Liberal Party, which had won sixty-six seats in the 1868 election, lost its near-monopoly of Irish representation. For the first time the Irish people's views were properly represented in Parliament. In the 1885 election the IPP, with Church support, won eighty-five seats, including seventeen in Ulster and one in Liverpool. This represented a landslide for Home Rule outside Ulster, where Unionists dominated. Not one Liberal member was elected in Ireland. Mass politics had emerged in Ireland with sectarian divisions predominant. In 1885 the IPP voted with the Tories against the Liberal government and brought it down. In July 1885 the Conservative government under Lord Salisbury was, in its turn, brought down when the IPP changed sides over the issue of coercion in Ireland. IPP influence had now become decisive in British politics: the Irish nationalists were deciding who would rule the United Kingdom as a whole. It is interesting that during the debates in the Commons on the 1884 Reform Bill, many MPs had predicted that it would give the Irish Party the balance of power. Ireland was heavily over-represented in the Commons, with over a hundred seats, but the IPP would block any proposal to reduce the number.

During the years 1885–1922 the British political system entered a period of transition with the break-up of the Liberal Party, the rise of the Labour movement and the reshaping of the Conservative Party. Lord Salisbury backed the 1884 Reform Bill as a means of capitalizing on the urban working-class Tory vote, which would otherwise be swamped by the Liberals. It was an age of populist and, eventually, democratic politics, and the traditional parties had to try to find new identities to appeal to a wider electorate. New ideas were appearing and party unity was under threat as party leaders found it hard to contain competing groups. The Conservative and Liberal parties spanned two worlds; they had to cater for the rising mass electorate and at the same time acknowledge the continuing power of the great interest groups and families, which had earlier dominated them and still retained their influence, such as the Salisbury clan in the Tory Party and the Cavendishes in the Liberal Party. For both parties, the Irish question was at once an opportunity, a useful political weapon and a danger. It was an issue which the parties could not ignore, but which was a potential threat to their unity.

Personal factors were also important. W. E. Gladstone, after taking over the leadership of the Liberal Party in 1868, devoted considerable effort to the solution of the Irish question, which he saw as a moral issue. Under the influence of John Stuart Mill, he followed the notion of moral politics, a belief in the centrality of religious and moral considerations in political decision-making. Gladstone saw himself as the agent of morality in the world. He believed there was a God-given 'providential order in the world', which it was the duty of a political leader to strive towards. In his view the solution of the Irish problem was a necessary element in the creation of this order. Gladstone, like so many at the time, had a simplistic and one-sided view of Irish history based on some very tendentious sources: he saw certain aspects of the Union, especially the union of the Churches, as inherently evil. He also believed that concrete reforms, such as changes in land tenure to strengthen 'responsible' landlordism and eliminate tenants' grievances, would remove injustices and help preserve the Union, which he thought mutually beneficial to Britain and Ireland.

Gladstone had great self-confidence. He saw himself as specially appointed by God to solve the Irish question. He did not take advice from Dublin on what was actually happening but had a deep conviction that he enjoyed special knowledge of the issue. If public opinion was against what he knew to be correct, he believed it had to be manipulated. In his opinion, it was not the function of a leader to follow public opinion, which in any case was usually only the expression of the views of selfish vested interests. Such views, and the idea that there was divine sanction for what he was doing, could be very irritating indeed for those around him.

Gladstone began to put his ideas into practice soon after becoming Prime Minister. The disestablishment of the Anglican Church in Ireland in 1869 removed a major religious grievance. From then on, the main focus of nationalist activity was the land question, the ending of the power of landlords and the creation of a class of small landed proprietors. Gladstone tried to solve this issue by legislation. The Land Act of 1870 removed some of the grievances of some tenants, but it did not go far enough because it did not force landlords to sell land to tenants.

In 1880 the Liberals won the general election called by Disraeli on the issue of resisting concessions to Ireland, and Gladstone came back into power. In the same year, the leadership of the IPP was assumed by Charles Stewart Parnell, a Protestant landowner and MP for Meath, who had considerable charisma. He had earlier emerged as a prominent member of the activist wing of the IPP, which wanted to use obstruction tactics in Parliament to force concessions out of the government. He had connections with many different branches of the nationalist movement, including the Irish Republican Brotherhood and the Clan na Gael, which he brought together in his 'New Departure'. He based his movement on the National Land League established in 1879 in Mayo, which opposed the activities of graziers trying to clear tenants from their lands. In co-operation with the other Land League leader, Michael Davitt, an IRB member, he quickly assembled a growing mass base. [**DOCUMENT I**] Another economic recession hit Ireland after 1879, and a new potato blight. The League received its most active support from the class of rising tenant farmers who wanted to increase their holdings.

The land issue had great symbolic importance: not surprisingly, it was the subject of numerous myths, in particular that of the oppressive English landlord. In many cases the oppressor of tenants was in fact a substantial Irish landlord. This is an example of how nationalism acted as a cloak for self-seeking and a means of disguising divisions in Irish society. The myth was more important than the reality: the oppressive alien landlord was an ideal hate-figure, against whom groups with divergent interests could unite. The rural crisis of the late 1870s produced a rarely seen, if temporary, social unity in much of the Irish countryside. Similarly the independent small farmer living on his family farm became for many the ideal or genuine Irishman, conservative, devout and, unlike the rich and sophisticated or those living in cities, unaffected by the corrosive new ideas regrettably circulating in Ireland. This notion greatly influenced many of the writers in the Irish Literary Revival. It should be noted, however, that most of the leaders of the League were large farmers.

Parnell and Davitt successfully converted the land issue into a general political campaign for Home Rule by creating the National League as a mass nationalist organization to back the IPP. As a result, Home Rule became, for the majority of Catholic Irishmen, a gateway to Utopia, a perfect world of happiness and prosperity from which all problems would disappear. The League launched the so-called Land War, which lasted from 1879 to 1882, a campaign of rent strikes, boycotts and violence against landlords, their property and their agents. The government responded, as usual, with a mixture of repression and concession. The 1881 Coercion Act suspended Habeas Corpus, but a month later the government passed a new Land Law giving tenants the so-called 'three Fs': fair rents, fixity of tenure and free sale with compensation for any improvements carried out by the tenant. A land court was to fix fair rents. This extended the principle of state intervention in the tenant–landlord relationship.

The Land War forged close links between constitutional and physical-force nationalism and re-created the alliance between the Roman Catholic Church, which supported the tenants, and constitutional nationalism. The IPP supported the provision of public funds for Catholic schools. The Church wanted religiously separate education and resisted attempts by the government to defuse religious problems in Ireland, for example by setting up in 1850 the non-sectarian Queen's University with colleges in Galway, Belfast and Cork. Between 1871 and 1970, Catholics were forbidden by their Church from attending Queen's College, Belfast, or Trinity College, Dublin. As a result of the success of the Land League and the IPP and the link between the Church and constitutional nationalism, physical-force nationalism declined in importance until the early twentieth century.

The new Land Law, though generous in its provisions, did not end rural violence, in which local factors such as private quarrels often played a part. It was answered by the government with more repression, including the arrest of Davitt and Parnell. Eventually the government entered the so-called Kilmainham agreement with Parnell in April 1882, whereby he was released from Kilmainham gaol and agreed to try to stop the violence in return for an extension of the Land Law. Under its terms, the IPP would 'co-operate cordially' with the Liberals in carrying through reforms.

As in 1798, these promising developments were ruined by a single event, the Phoenix Park murders in May 1882. The new Chief Secretary for Ireland, Lord Frederick Cavendish, the younger son of the Duke of Devonshire and a man close to Gladstone – he was married to Mrs Gladstone's niece and was almost a son to him – and the chief under-secretary, Thomas Burke, were murdered in brutal circumstances by members of a small physical-force nationalist group, the Irish National Invincibles. The five men responsible were eventually betrayed and hanged. In turn, the informer who had betrayed them was murdered while sailing to a new life in South Africa. His murderer, eventually executed, was seen as a martyr for Ireland.

The murders probably set back Irish Home Rule for twenty years. They caused a new wave of revulsion against the Irish in Britain, reflected for example in the cartoons in *Punch*. The Irish were no longer portrayed as figures of fun but as simian subhumans carrying daggers dripping blood. The Phoenix Park murders also coincided with a growing wave of imperialist emotion in Britain caused by intervention in the Sudan, which culminated in the death of General

Gordon at Khartoum in 1885. Public opinion in Britain turned sharply against Irish Home Rule. As a result, the Liberal Party was unable to deploy propaganda in its favour. In June 1885 a minority Conservative government came to power with IPP support in return for promises of reform in Ireland.

A further development came with the so-called Hawarden Kite in December 1885, named after Gladstone's country estate in Flintshire. Gladstone was very keen to remove the IPP from Westminster because it was distorting the British political process, and he had a genuine hope that a bipartisan policy would be possible. He would have preferred the Conservative Party to introduce Home Rule, as it would be better able to carry it through the Lords. At Hawarden, Gladstone's son Herbert, without any authority and without making it clear that he was talking 'off the record', declared his father's conversion to Home Rule, while talking to reporters. This disastrous leak ended any chance that the Irish question might be settled by consensus between the two main British parties. The Conservative Party, convinced that Gladstone was double-dealing, now refused to entertain the idea. It was also eager to jump on the rising popular imperialist bandwagon as a way of adapting to the new age of mass politics, which threatened the party with extinction. For the next thirty years, therefore, the Irish question became a football in party politics.

The murders also had a major impact on British politics. By preventing a rapid solution of the Irish question, they effectively kept Gladstone as leader of the Liberal Party until 1894. He was keen to withdraw from political life, but the Irish question prevented him from doing so: he was unwilling to retire until he had settled Ireland because he believed that he alone was capable of solving the problem. He also hoped to hold together the Liberal Party by giving it a great moral issue around which it could unite. His remaining in office blocked the rise of Joseph Chamberlain, a leading radical Liberal seen by many as Gladstone's heir apparent. There was also a personal factor: Gladstone was very keen to stop radicals like Chamberlain and Charles Dilke, who supported the disestablishment of the Anglican Church and a form of radical populist Liberalism, embodied for example in the 'Unauthorized Programme' of 1885, of which Gladstone very strongly disapproved. Chamberlain had earlier involved himself in Irish affairs on the side of Home Rule and now put forward his Central Board scheme, involving devolution for Ireland, as an alternative to Home Rule. He was also becoming an increasingly strong supporter of the British Empire as an institution. Chamberlain was a man of fierce

convictions, which he kept changing. His ambition shone from him
like an aura, and he was very ruthless. He wanted to head a radical
government with no old Whigs and moderates to put the brakes on
his far-reaching schemes. There is some suspicion that he was involved
in bringing about the divorce cases which toppled Dilke in 1886 and
Parnell in 1890, both of whom stood in his way.

Frustrated in his ambitions, Chamberlain turned against Home Rule
during 1885 and 1886. He now saw his future in a new political
movement, Liberal Unionism. In this he was joined by the Marquess
of Hartington, brother of the murdered Lord Frederick Cavendish.
Hartington was highly regarded by fellow politicians, including opponents, as a man of conviction and honesty. They and their allies were
able to block Home Rule. In 1886 the Liberal Party split, with the
Liberal Unionists going into alliance with the Conservatives. Apart
from their landslide victory of 1906, the years 1885 to 1910 saw a
decline in the Liberal share of the vote, and the party was only saved
from disaster by temporary factors such as an alliance with the IPP,
which, of course, had the price-tag of continuing commitment to Irish
Home Rule.

In 1886 Gladstone announced his intention to bring in a Home
Rule Bill. This involved a very limited devolution of power to an
Irish Parliament but would have removed all the Irish MPs from
Westminster. The powers of the Irish Parliament were vague and ill
defined; the bill merely laid down restrictions on them by defining the
reserved powers of the imperial Parliament. The financial provisions
in the bill were ill thought out and the cost to the British Exchequer
would have been huge. The whole thing was imprecise, and it is hard
to see how it could have worked in practice. Even this bloodless form
of devolution provoked Unionist opposition, but Gladstone was very
firm in his view that the Unionist minority in Ulster did not have
any right to veto the Home Rule desired by a majority of the Irish
electorate. He was also convinced that, faced with a *fait accompli*, they
would eventually accept it.

This first Home Rule Bill led to the emergence of organized Ulster
Unionism and produced the split in the Liberal Party described
above. The Liberal Unionists voted with the Tories, who saw the
bill as legitimizing Irish crime by giving in to violence. Gladstone's
government fell in June 1886 with the defeat of the bill. In July
Lord Salisbury came back as Prime Minister. The Conservatives and
Unionists were to rule from 1886 until 1906 with a brief Liberal
government from August 1892 to June 1895, when Gladstone came

back as Prime Minister and in 1893 introduced another Home Rule Bill, this time retaining some Irish MPs at Westminster. Again this was thrown out in the House of Lords. Gladstone finally resigned in March 1894.

The failures of 1886 and 1893 made the Irish problem much worse. The Home Rule Bills roused the appetites of the Nationalists without satisfying them, and badly frightened the Unionists. They also initiated a period of instability in British political life, which made a solution much more difficult. Gladstone was guilty of gross miscalculation: he expected the Tories to do their duty by helping the bill through, but his hopes for a bipartisan policy on the Irish issue were totally unrealistic. Lord Salisbury declared that the Irish, like Hottentots, were incapable of self-government.

Another element of instability appeared with the fall of Parnell in 1891 after a scandal over his long-standing love affair with Mrs O'Shea, the wife of a fellow IPP Member. Most of Parnell's party colleagues deserted him after he came under joint attack from Gladstone and the Catholic Church in Ireland. It would be wrong to exaggerate the damage this did to the party – the legend quickly grew up of Parnell as the lost aristocratic leader succeeded by pygmies – but certainly the Irish Party became divided following his fall until it revived under John Redmond's leadership post-1900. The traditional view, that the period after 1891 was politically stagnant and that the main impetus in nationalist activity passed to cultural and linguistic groups, is too simple. The 1890s saw a revival of agrarian agitation, with the appearance in 1898 of the United Irish League, which preached Home Rule as well as land reform, though the urgency seemed to have gone out of the issue. The IPP was able to gain further concessions from the government, and it retained the support of the Catholic clergy.

Between 1886 and 1905 successive Conservative governments refused to make any concessions on Home Rule. Plans for devolution in 1904–5 were dropped in the face of Unionist opposition. Between 1905 and 1916 the Tory Party was dominated by Irish Unionist opinion. The British electorate had other concerns and politicians' apparent obsession with the Irish issue was increasingly resented. The government revived a policy of trying to kill Irish nationalism by kindness, a policy which came to be known as 'constructive Unionism'. Arthur Balfour, Chief Secretary for Ireland from 1887 to 1891, played a major role in this. His rigorous enforcement of the law earned him the nickname 'Bloody Balfour' in Ireland, but he was equally determined to redress legitimate grievances. The measures enacted amounted to a revolution from above or 'a slow revolution by legislation', and they forced the IPP to look for another issue, apart from the land question, to mobilize support. The measures included a new Land Act (1887), giving tenants wider security of tenure and establishing a government fund to enable them to buy the freeholds of their lands on mortgages with repayments lower than the original rents. In 1891 a third Land Act made available even more generous grants. There were large investments in work-creation schemes run by the Congested Districts Board, and new railways were built to link the west to the east. In 1903 a further Land Act was passed. Under it, by 1921 the government had spent £100 million to enable 250,000 tenants to buy their land. The power of the landlords was broken and a society of independent small farmers was created in Ireland.

The land reforms were accompanied by educational reforms which established a comprehensive Catholic education system. The sweeping 1898 Local Government Act extended democratic local government to Ireland. Women had the vote in local elections. The county and district councils elected under this Act provided a good training ground for the next generation of Irish politicians.

These concessions did not end demands for Home Rule. Indeed, they made the whole problem worse because, by removing concrete grievances, they concentrated attention on the issue of Home Rule for its own sake. These years saw a major revival of nationalism in Ireland. During the 1890s many older nationalist writings, for example, on 1848 and the Young Ireland movement, were reprinted, providing a new generation of young people with new heroes. The Gaelic revival played a major role in all this. In 1884 the Gaelic Athletic Association (GAA) was set up to promote a revival of traditional Irish sports. There was a considerable IRB element in this from the outset, and it was overtly political and very anti-English. In 1893 the Gaelic League was established by Douglas Hyde, a Protestant, and Eoin MacNeill, a noted historian. The stated aim of the League was to revive the dying Irish language, the weak state of which was revealed by the census of 1891; but a subsidiary objective of its upper middle-class leaders was the rescue of the nationalist movement from the hands of riff-raff. They sought to provide an alternative to Catholicism around which the Irish could cohere, and to create a nationalism which was not rooted in self-seeking and jobbery but in the heroic past and its culture. Culture and language provided an alternative focus for the attention of nationalists, especially urban middle-class youth. The IRB joined the Gaelic League *en masse*, though, like the GAA, it was supposed to be non-political and non-sectarian. In 1900 the first edition of its paper, *The Leader*, contained a letter from W. B. Yeats stating that, whereas in the past the land had been the engine of nationalism, in the future it would be the language issue. This was not in fact true, because the language revival movement attracted no more than a small though very enthusiastic minority. The League was able to obtain concessions on the language question from the government, for example, the introduction in 1906 of Irish as a subject in schools.

In 1905 Sinn Féin (Ourselves) was set up under Arthur Griffith and Bulmer Hobson as a new political party concentrating on county council elections. At its foundation it was a constitutional nationalist movement with close links with the cultural revivalists. At first it went through a very bleak period and was deeply divided until it was revived by its Belfast members. There was also a growing mobilization of women in the nationalist movement, culminating in 1913 in the establishment of the republican Cumann Na mBan. In 1898, the centenary of the 1798 rising was the occasion for a great mobilization of anti-British sentiment. The Boer War also roused anti-British feeling as Irish Nationalists came out in support of the Boers. The rhetoric used was violent but very rarely translated into action. Revolutionary nationalism was weak in these years and police reports of the period suggested that the extremists had very little support.

3.   Deepening Divisions, 1906–1916

In the years before the First World War, the Irish question entered a critical phase. Although Britain seemed at the zenith of its power, there was an atmosphere of unease and impending trouble in the country. A large section of the British political élite had lost its mid-Victorian confidence. Lord Salisbury, an archetypal representative of the landowning aristocracy still so prominent in the ruling élite, increasingly bewailed the decline of traditional values and the advance of materialism and class conflict, which threatened to destroy the world as he knew it. British political life was becoming starkly polarized over a range of different issues, including labour unrest, the militant suffragettes' agitation, independence movements in the Empire and an increasingly threatening international situation. The country seemed to be dividing into two camps, the party of progress and the party of stability, confronting one another in deepening hostility and sharing less and less common ground.

The rise of the Left was seen by many as particularly threatening. The Parliament elected in 1906 contained fifty-nine Labour and 'Lib-Lab' MPs. There was growing labour unrest, especially in the new mass unions of unskilled workers. The years 1911 to 1912 saw a wave of strikes, about 860 in all. There was a real fear of a general strike and of Continental anarchy or anarcho-syndicalism spreading to Britain. There were genuine fears of an attempt to overturn the constitution by violence. In these circumstances Ireland came to occupy a position of symbolic significance. For the Left, in the broadest sense, Home Rule for Ireland represented a victory of justice and principle over self-interest; for the Right, the fight of the Ulster Unionists against Home Rule was a defence of traditional British values under attack on all fronts.

In the 1906 election the Liberals won a landslide victory over a Conservative Party discredited and divided on the issue of tariff reform. The new government, which could be described as the first British government of the Left, proposed sweeping changes, including the creation of a welfare state. The Tories made it clear that they would block measures they disapproved of. The new government's plans to introduce major social and other reforms soon came up against a determined rearguard action by the defenders of the established order in the House of Lords, where there was an inbuilt Conservative majority. The policies proposed by the Liberals inspired a political bitterness the like of which had rarely been experienced. In spite of major reforms, such as the Haldane army reforms, the introduction of old age pensions and the establishment of labour exchanges, the government lost public support rapidly. As a result, the Opposition was able to argue that the government did not have a mandate for what it was proposing.

Most Liberals accepted that Irish Home Rule was inevitable but wanted to avoid it for as long as they could, being well aware of the potential dangers in the issue. After 1906, the Liberal Prime Minister, Campbell-Bannerman, tried to find some form of devolution which would satisfy the Nationalists and be acceptable to the Unionists, but his 1907 Irish Councils bill did not go far enough, and the Nationalists returned to a policy of disrupting the Commons. By this time the influence of Unionism was so great that it was able to obtain binding promises from a number of British governments, which eventually led to the partition of Ireland.

According to one historian of Unionism, Patrick Buckland: 'It is difficult to exaggerate the importance of Irish unionism for British and Irish politics in the late nineteenth and early twentieth centuries.' It became a serious political movement from the 1880s. There were basically two forms of Unionism, one in Ulster and one in southern Ireland, and they were very different. In Ulster it grew into a kind of mass nationalism and had a major impact on developments in the province. The identification of Irish nationalism with Catholicism and Gaelicism fostered the growth of a distinct Ulster identity based on the Protestant religion, the British way of life and the maintenance of the Union of Ireland and Britain. The strength of Ulster Unionism lay in two factors, the simplicity of its ideas and the robustness of its methods. It was also based on a deep conviction of the innate superiority of Protestantism over Catholicism. These attitudes have changed little in 200 years.

The origins of the movement lay in the late eighteenth century. At that time Ulster was becoming economically distinct from the rest of Ireland. It was much more prosperous, largely as a result of a thriving linen industry, and a substantial Presbyterian middle class grew up. From the 1770s there were clear signs of growing religious confrontation in Ulster. Sectarian terrorist gangs appeared, drawing on the long-established tradition of rural secret societies, which had begun in Ulster and spread to other parts of Ireland. The main terrorist groups in Ulster were the Peep O'Day Boys, who were Protestants, and the Defenders, who were Catholics. Tithes were a major grievance fuelling this development, and in the late eighteenth century growing land hunger, caused by a sharp population rise, began to exacerbate religious differences. The Catholic Relief Act of 1793 aroused further fears among Protestants. In September 1795 the two groups fought a major battle at the Diamond in Armagh, which was won by the Protestants. This confrontation led directly to the foundation of the Loyal Orange Order, a masonic organization devoted to the defence of Protestantism and loyalty to the Crown. The Order grew rapidly after the 1798 rising, which was seen in Ulster as a Catholic pogrom. Ironically, many Protestants opposed the Union of 1801 out of fear that it would lead to Catholic emancipation, and Orangeism began as an anti-Unionist movement. This soon changed.

The enactment of Catholic emancipation in 1829 provoked a wave of sectarian violence in Ulster. A significant development was growing solidarity between the different Protestant sects when earlier there had been deep hostility. The 1850 Franchise Act tightened up the regulations on who could vote, enlarging the rural and reducing the urban electorate. This produced an incentive for the Unionists to consolidate their political organization where they were strong. In the process, the sectarian political division was deepened.

In its early stages Unionism placed great emphasis on the vital link with Britain as a guarantee of religious and civil liberties and of economic prosperity. Ulster was growing away from Ireland. The Anglican, landowning ruling class used fear of the Catholics as a useful means of diverting the social grievances of the Protestant poor from themselves – an important matter as Ulster also suffered during the economic recessions of the 1820s and 1840s. This was always a feature of Ulster Unionism: the mobilization of support for the Union across the classes was a convenient method of destroying working-class solidarity and a means of social control. Religious solidarity between employer and employee was a useful weapon against socialism, though there was an organized labour movement among working-class Protestants in Ulster, which was not immune from strikes. There were, for example, serious dock strikes in Belfast in 1907 and 1908 and an attempt, in the Independent Orange Institution established in 1902, to combine Unionism and socialism. It would be over-simple to see Unionism as simply the exploitation of irrational fears in defence of the vested interests of the possessing classes. The weakness of the socialist element in Irish Nationalism was the other side of the coin: Catholic property owners in the South also found Nationalism a convenient means of diverting the attention of the poor from their real interests.

The Orange Order, after a period of stagnation, was refounded in 1845 specifically to organize Protestant working-class loyalism in response to a revival of Irish Nationalism. Unionism grew rapidly during the Land War of the late 1870s, when Orange workers were organized to break boycotts organized by the Land League in Ulster and neighbouring counties. The violence of the Land Leaguers was often answered by Unionist violence. In 1885 the Irish Loyal and Patriotic Union was set up in Dublin to put up anti-Home Rule candidates in elections. The Irish Unionist Party was established in 1886 when Gladstone introduced the first Home Rule Bill. Its first leader was a former Conservative MP, Colonel Edward J. Sanderson, the author of *Two Irelands: Or Loyalty versus Treason* (1884). In the 1880s there were anti-Home Rule riots in Belfast, a revival of Unionism where it had been declining before, and a sharp increase in the membership of the Orange Order. Unionism quickly became a mass movement. About 75 per cent of the population of Belfast were Protestants, and they were totally dominant in the shipbuilding and engineering industries. Home Rule was seen as a threat not only to religious and civil liberties but also to the economy of Ulster. [**DOCUMENT II**] It was also seen as a threat to the security of the British Isles: a collection of essays published in London in 1912, *Against Home Rule: The Case for the Union*, edited by S. Rosenbaum, emphasized the military and naval threat which an independent Ireland would represent for Britain. In 1891 the Irish Unionist Alliance was established with an aristocratic leadership, centred in southern Ireland and devoted to constitutional methods. In 1907 a Joint Committee of Irish Unionist Associations was set up as a co-ordinating body. This was in control by 1912, by which time the Ulster Unionist Council, led by men committed to more robust methods, had total dominance over the movement. Almost from the beginning, the Ulster Unionist MPs made it clear that, if constitutional methods failed, they would resist Home Rule by force. Constitutional and physical-force Nationalism were therefore mirrored in Unionism.

By 1912 the British political scene had undergone changes which considerably enhanced the influence of the Unionists. In 1909 a major political crisis broke when Asquith, who became Prime Minister in 1908, called a general election on a constitutional issue after the House of Lords, on 30 November 1909, threw out the reforming 'People's Budget' of Lloyd George, Chancellor of the Exchequer since 1908. A radical Liberal strongly opposed to privilege and committed to social reform, Lloyd George was hated by the Tories because of the deliberately provocative language of his speeches and his pro-Boer stance during the South African War. His 1909 budget, designed, as he said, to 'wage warfare against poverty and squalidness', introduced a land tax, death duties and new excise duties to fund a range of social reforms and a larger navy. The Chancellor's speeches in favour of his budget were full of appeals to class hatred, and it was deliberately designed to provoke a confrontation with the Lords, whose earlier blocking of reforms enraged many Liberals. The Tories saw it, as was intended, as an attack on property and on the constitution, and they therefore breached the unwritten constitutional rule, unbroken for over two centuries, that the Lords did not interfere with finance bills. For them the House of Lords was the last bastion of a fortress being eaten away by the tides of change. Its powers had to be preserved at all costs.

In the election held in January 1910 the Liberals lost heavily, sacrificing 104 seats. The constitutional issue of peers versus people did not ignite great popular enthusiasm; rather the electorate was motivated by disappointment over the government's failure to fulfil many of its promises and by the belief that it was soft on defence. Arthur Balfour's prediction in 1906 that the Liberal Party would collapse because it would be too radical for the propertied classes and not radical enough for labour seemed to be coming true. The party leaders' campaigning before the election seemed to lack energy, showing signs of the exhaustion caused by the constitutional crisis.

In the new House of Commons the Liberals had 275 seats, the Conservatives 273, Labour 40 and the IPP 82. The IPP therefore held the balance and Asquith agreed to introduce a new Home Rule Bill as the price of their support for a Liberal government. The political scene was in a state of flux. The government wished to weaken the Lords but was uncertain how to achieve this. Whatever course was chosen, it was very likely that the Lords' consent would only be obtained by packing the House with Liberal peers. At the opening of Parliament in 1910 King Edward VII said that legislation would be introduced to define the relationship between the two Houses. Eventually three measures were put forward, abolishing the Lords' veto of money bills, enacting that the Lords' veto would lapse if the Commons passed a measure three times in successive parliamentary sessions, and reducing the life of each Parliament from seven to five years. These measures, the Parliament Bill, were passed by the Commons in April. Asquith then threatened the resignation of his government if it did not become law. In reality the Liberal Party was not ready to risk another general election on the issue unless it had guarantees that, if it won, measures would be taken to ensure the passage of the bill even against the Lords' opposition. Asquith assured the House of Commons on 14 April 1910 that he would obtain the necessary guarantees. Clearly what was involved here was the exercise of the royal prerogatives to dissolve Parliament and to create peers.

On the King's suggestion, twenty-one meetings of a constitutional conference of four Liberals and four Conservatives were held between 17 June and 11 November to try to arrive at an acceptable compromise. During the course of it Lloyd George, without the Prime Minister's knowledge, suggested a grand coalition government to solve the constitutional and Irish issues, to carry through social reform and to bring in conscription, a very sensitive issue. Balfour rejected this. Throughout the negotiations the Irish question seemed to be pushed into the background. The IPP, on which the government depended, became increasingly annoyed at what they saw as an attempt by the British Establishment to gang up against them. In fact, the constitutional conference failed, largely over the question of Irish Home Rule, which had become an issue of principle for the Conservatives and Unionists. On 16 November 1910 Asquith asked the King for a promise to create anything up to 500 peers if the Lords threw out the Parliament Bill and Parliament was dissolved. Otherwise he threatened that the government would resign at once. George V, who had only recently succeeded to the throne, much against the advice he received from many quarters and against his own better judgement, gave a confidential promise. The main object was to save Asquith's position.

A second general election in 1910, held in December, brought little change. The Liberals and Conservatives won 272 seats each, the Irish 84 and the Labour Party 42. However, it could now be argued that a majority of the electorate desired constitutional change. In the event, the creation of peers was not necessary. The Lords eventually abandoned their opposition to the changes, but a dubious precedent had been established which threatened the constitutional impartiality of the Crown. The whole episode sharpened party antagonisms because there was a suspicion that the government had offended constitutional proprieties. In July 1911 Asquith revealed the existence of the King's undertaking to create peers to the leader of the Conservatives, Balfour, who was outraged that he had not been asked to form a government. The Parliament Bill was again debated. In July there were attempts in the Lords to alter it by, for example, laying down that any proposal to grant Home Rule to Ireland, Scotland or Wales should be approved by a referendum of the electorate. This led to a great hardening of attitudes among the Unionists. There were ugly scenes in the Commons on 24 July, when the Conservatives howled down Asquith and the Speaker had to adjourn the House. In August the Lords passed a vote of censure against the government concerning the King's undertaking. The King also received a large number of letters, accusing him, among other things, of betraying the Irish Unionists. The situation became even worse when it was revealed that Redmond, the leader of the IPP, had demanded a promise to create peers to ensure the passage of a Home Rule Bill through the Lords as the price for continued IPP support of the government. This raised the possibility that any other minority party which held the balance of power in the Commons might obtain promises from the Crown to ensure the attainment of its wishes and made inter-party consensus on the Irish issue even more remote.

The Lords passed the Parliament Bill on 10 August 1911 after a statement was read repeating the King's intention to create peers if necessary. The Act limited the Lords' veto power and promised in the preamble a reform of the House of Lords to make it more democratic. This has never been carried out; the House of Commons has been far too worried about creating a real rival to its own power. Discussion of proportional representation also came to nothing: the old single-member first-past-the-post system was seen by most MPs as a barrier to the growth of a dangerous third party, in this case the Labour Party.

In the mean time, growing impatience in Ireland had led to the emergence of a more extreme Nationalist movement. In 1910 Sinn Féin split, and from it emerged a physical-force group under the Ulster Nationalist, Bulmer Hobson. At first, it was marginal because the IPP seemed to be winning Home Rule, which was all the great majority in southern Ireland wanted.

In February 1910 the Unionist Party acquired an energetic new leader in the person of the Dublin lawyer, Sir Edward Carson, and it too became more extreme. Carson was born in Dublin and lived there until he was 40. He always regarded himself as an Irishman, but he believed that Ireland's place was in the Empire. Carson became an extremely popular figure in Britain and came to enjoy a respect among the public not shared by many politicians. His first major achievement was to persuade the Unionists in different parts of Ireland to sink their differences. From the outset he made it clear that he intended to combat Home Rule by constitutional means, but behind this there was always the threat of violence. In September 1911 the party issued the Craigavon Declaration, containing the threat to establish a separate Ulster government in Belfast if Home Rule were forced through. The following year, on 28 September, there took place the signing of the Ulster Solemn League and Covenant in ceremonies all over the province. The signatories pledged themselves to resist Home Rule by all means. This was followed by the setting up of a provisional government to take over Ulster on the day Home Rule was declared. In January 1913 the Ulster Volunteer Force was set up, a private army of over 100,000 men, regularly drilled with the help of British officers, under Lord Roberts of Kandahar. In April 1914 guns bought in Germany were landed at Larne to arm the Volunteers. The example of the Unionists might be copied in the South, and these events severely weakened the moderate Nationalists and strengthened the physical-force group.

The Unionists tried to justify their actions by appeals to a perversion of seventeenth-century contract theories: that rebellion against a government failing in its duty to its subjects was legitimate. The Ulster Unionist Council stated in 1912: 'It is incompetent for any authority, party or people to appoint as our rulers a government dominated by men disloyal to the empire and to whom our faith and traditions are hateful.' Home Rule was 'the most nefarious conspiracy that has ever been hatched against a free people'. In spite of such arguments, the whole business was, in reality, treasonable and illegal. Some ministers in the government wanted to prosecute the Unionist leaders, but the majority were unwilling or frightened to confront the movement. They preferred to ignore it in the hope that it would go away. Redmond also advised the government against provoking the Unionists. Of course, if the government failed to take action against Unionist traitors, could it then take action against Nationalist traitors? In the government only the First Lord of the Admiralty, Winston Churchill, urged firm action against Ulster but his colleagues were too nervous. Churchill was eventually forced out of the government in 1915 when the Unionists demanded this as the price of joining a coalition government with the Liberals.

Something of the 'garrison psychology' which had always affected the behaviour of the Ulster planters was exported from Ireland to Britain and began to affect those who saw their interests and values threatened by the trends of the age. Even some who had earlier supported a measure of Home Rule as a means of removing grievances and rendering Ireland safe sympathized with the Ulster cause. Many British people regarded the aspirations of the Irish nationalists with incomprehension and contempt, especially when it became known that they were supported by foreign powers unfavourable to Britain (for example, Germany). Many saw the granting of Home Rule to Ireland as the thin end of the wedge. A kind of domino theory might operate: Home Rule for Ireland would give a dreadful example to other subject lands like India and Egypt, and might threaten the existence of the whole British Empire, a haloized structure which had had new life breathed into it by the ceremonial around Queen Victoria's Diamond Jubilee in 1897. An important manifestation of the late Victorian crisis of confidence was jingoism, a demonstrative, popular mass imperialism. Extreme British nationalism manifested itself in the Sudanese troubles in the 1880s, the Boer War and the Irish question. Imperial ideology and culture were all-pervasive. There was a fear of weakening Britain at a time when the war-clouds were gathering in Europe. There was also deeply rooted anti-Catholic feeling among wide sections of the British people, and this produced a genuine fear of the 'Rome Rule' which, the Unionists claimed, would be an inevitable consequence of Home Rule. The Irish Unionists were seen as guardians of good old values, and their courageous resistance against plans to rob them of their British heritage was widely applauded. Other developments strengthened these fears. King George V refused to give the usual Protestant Declaration, customary since the 1678 Popish Plot, when opening his first Parliament. The traditional version of this contained very anti-Catholic statements. Instead the King gave a simple declaration that he was a Protestant and would uphold the Protestant succession. This was seen as evidence of the baleful influence of Papists in the highest places. The king's coronation oath to uphold the Protestant religion was quoted: did he have the right to place some of his subjects under Catholic rule at the request of a government without a clear majority in either house of Parliament?

The Conservatives used the Ulster issue to increase their political power and as a means of rescuing the party from what some saw as its inevitable decline because of the rise of a mass electorate and socialism. Also, many British peers had land in Ireland, including very influential figures like the Duke of Devonshire and the Marquess of Lansdowne. Lord Salisbury saw the Unionist alliance as a device which would enable his party to survive as a party of government even in an era of popular politics. The Conservative alliance with the Unionists is said to have been sealed in February 1886 when Lord Randolph Churchill, a prominent Conservative politician, went to Belfast and 'played the Orange card', promising his party's support for the cause. The significance of this event has sometimes been distorted: at that time the Ulster Unionists were seeking to use the Conservatives for their political ends and not vice versa. Churchill's speech on that occasion was very moderate and did not contain the famous words 'Ulster will fight and Ulster will be right!' later attributed to it. They were written later. His aim at that point seemed to be to encourage Unionism among Irish Catholics. The speech did not, in fact, create the Orange factor in British politics; support for the Union had been part of the Tory consciousness for most of the nineteenth century and was not something which appeared only in 1886.

The new Conservative leader from November 1911, after Arthur Balfour resigned, was Andrew Bonar Law. A rather colourless compromise candidate, he was the son of an Ulster Protestant emigrant to Canada and sympathized deeply with the Unionist cause. On 27 July 1912 he spoke to a great Tory gathering at Blenheim Palace in support of Ulster. At the same meeting the Duke of Norfolk presented Carson with a golden sword with which to defend the Union.

In April 1912 Asquith introduced the third Irish Home Rule Bill. This proposed the establishment of a two-chamber all-Ireland Parliament in Dublin with limited authority over internal affairs. As critics said, it was little more than a glorified county council. Foreign policy, defence and financial matters were to remain under the control of the Westminster Parliament, to which forty-two Irish MPs would continue to be elected. This bill was passed in the Commons in 1912, 1913 and 1914 and each time it was thrown out in the Lords by the built-in Conservative and Unionist majority. Opponents argued that Asquith did not have a mandate for such a major constitutional change because he could pass Acts only with IPP support. Asquith's deal with Redmond after the 1910 election was seen as a corrupt bargain to keep a minority government in power, and many believed a general election should be held on the Irish issue. The King wanted this, but Asquith warned that the Crown would become the football of factions if Parliament were dissolved against the advice of ministers. Accusations circulated that the Liberals had precipitated the death of Edward VII by pressurizing him on the Parliament Bill. Unionists urged the King to withhold his consent from the Home Rule Bill on the grounds that it would lead to civil war in Ireland. They claimed that the Liberals, by extracting the promise to create peers, had brought the Crown into the party struggle and that they could now legitimately do the same. In November 1912 Bonar Law proposed that the Unionists should pursue a policy of deliberate disruption of Parliament to stop Home Rule, and that month saw frequent outbursts of violence, leading to suspensions of the House. It was clear that deep divisions were again opening up in the Commons and that the Opposition was trying to force the calling of a general election on the Irish issue. The King, however, was unwilling to dismiss a government which could still command a clear majority in the Commons.

The possibility of finding a compromise solution based on the partition of Ireland was under discussion from 1911. The exclusion of areas of Ireland with Protestant majorities, the four counties of Antrim, Armagh, Londonderry and Down, from Home Rule was first suggested on 11 June 1912 by Mr Robartes, MP for St Austell, during the committee stage of the Home Rule Bill in the Commons. Sir Edward Carson, the leader of the Ulster Unionists, suggested the addition of Tyrone and Fermanagh, which had substantial Protestant minorities. The King was increasingly convinced that a temporary exclusion of Ulster was the only way out of a nasty constitutional impasse. This view was clearly stated in a letter from the King to Asquith on 22 September 1913. Secret conversations about the Ulster option were held between Bonar Law and Asquith in October 1913. When news of these leaked out, it again raised fears in both the Nationalist and Unionist camps that the Establishment was trying to go behind their backs. Eventually, early in 1914, Redmond was persuaded by Lloyd George and Augustine Birrell, Chief Secretary for Ireland from 1907 to 1916, to agree to a temporary exclusion of Ulster from Home Rule, but Carson would not accept a time limit on the exclusion. [**DOCUMENT III**] Others tried to find an answer in a general devolution plan to give Home Rule to Ulster, Southern Ireland, Scotland, Wales and England, with an imperial parliament looking after common matters. This plan came to nothing.

By March 1914 the British government was considering the possibility of military action to enforce the Home Rule Bill in Ulster. General Nevil Macready, a military commander already experienced in dealing with industrial unrest in south Wales, was appointed to Dublin with a 'dormant commission' as Military Governor of Belfast. Macready was a sensible and moderate *politique* general, who gave the government good advice, though he was not always heeded. News of these preparations precipitated an event of major significance, the so-called Curragh Mutiny in March 1914. General Sir Arthur Paget was sent to Ireland with orders to reinforce stores and depots in Ulster in case of attempts to seize them during an insurrection. Orders were also given to a number of destroyers to move to Ulster waters as part of precautionary measures in case it became necessary to contain an armed rising in the province. It has subsequently been revealed that a number of naval officers were ready to hand their ships over to an Ulster provisional government. Paget exaggerated the significance of these preparations, portraying them as the first stages of armed action to coerce Ulster into acceptance of Home Rule. Troops at the Curragh garrison 30 miles outside Dublin were ordered to be ready to march, but there was no clarity about exactly what the army was to do. Blundering behaviour by Paget led, on 20 March, to a 'mutiny' led by Brigadier-General Sir Hubert Gough, during which the officers stated that they would resign their commissions rather than accept orders to march north to coerce Ulster.

This event was followed by ten days of near-chaos in government circles in London. The war minister, Seeley, the chief of staff, Sir Henry Wilson, and the army commander, Sir John French, without government approval, gave assurances to Gough that the government would under no circumstances order the army to enforce Home Rule in Ulster. Wilson was an Ulsterman and an ardent Unionist, who is said to have kept Carson informed of military arrangements to deal with Ulster. There was a real fear of splitting the army from top to bottom at a time of mounting international tension, even of civil war in Britain over Ireland. It was said that the use of force to defeat the Ulster Volunteers could take between twelve and eighteen months and would need the entire British army. The country seemed close to total constitutional breakdown. Many believed that the government was drifting and did not know what to do about Ulster.

This was probably correct. In reality, no one knew what to do. Perhaps some in the government hoped that a show of force would deter the Unionists from taking action. It is probable that, given concerted pressure, Carson would have accepted the option for the four north-eastern counties with Protestant majorities (Antrim, Down, Londonderry and Armagh), which, it was believed, would not have been viable as a political entity alone. There was some doubt how far Carson could control the more extreme Unionists, who were clearly thinking of a permanent Protestant state in north-eastern Ireland and wanted to include Fermanagh, Tyrone and Derry city, which had Catholic majorities, for strategic and emotional reasons. Enniskillen in Fermanagh and the city of Derry were the sites of Protestant victories in the seventeenth century. Also unresolved was the question of the length of the exclusion of Ulster from Home Rule once the government had accepted the principle of exclusion in 1914. The government was thinking in terms of six years, while Carson wanted a permanent exclusion. Redmond optimistically believed that, when it came to it, Ulster would come into a Home Rule Ireland in return for special guarantees. The Nationalists did not regard the Ulster question as the most important issue at stake, and most did not, apparently, take Unionism very seriously.

The government's resolve was weakened by a belief that the army was unreliable. When Asquith tried to withdraw the unauthorized promise of Wilson and French to Gough, French and the war minister, Seeley, resigned. Asquith had to take over as Secretary of State for War. This was followed by a threat of mass resignation by military officers, who were overwhelmingly Unionist in sympathy. It was known that the King was very concerned about the prospect and was putting pressure on the government. The situation was made worse when the Lord Chancellor, Haldane, announced in the House of Lords that 'no orders were issued, no orders are likely to be issued and no orders will be issued for the coercion of Ulster' and later tried to have the word 'immediate' inserted before 'coercion' in *Hansard*. In the sensitive circumstances of the time, this provoked an outcry. In May 1914 the Home Rule Bill was passed in the House of Commons for the third time, with an additional provision giving the Protestant counties the chance to opt out for six years. In the Lords this was amended to give the whole of Ulster – nine counties – a permanent opt-out. Between 21 and 24 July 1914 a constitutional conference at Buckingham Palace, called on the initiative of the King, failed to find a compromise. The main point at issue was the exact boundary of the 'Ulster' which was to be excluded from Home Rule. Certain areas, the city of Derry, South Down, South Armagh, Fermanagh and Tyrone, had Catholic majorities.

On 4 August Britain went to war with Germany. The outbreak of war probably came as a relief to the government, as it promoted national unity and shelved the Irish issue. When the royal assent was given to the Home Rule Bill on 15 September, the clause on the exclusion of Ulster was suspended but the government issued a promise to pass an amending Act to cater for Ulster when the Act came into operation. All parties agreed to a suspension of the Act until the end of the war. Unfortunately, the question was to be much radicalized by developments during the First World War, which made an acceptable compromise solution even more difficult to find.

Some Irish Nationalists were not ready to wait until the end of the war to be given their country's freedom and determined to seize it by force. As a result, the Irish national state was born in blood. An active Nationalist and later a minister in the Irish government, Kevin O'Higgins, was to write of 'a weird composite of idealism, neurosis, megalomania and criminality' brought to the surface by the revolutionary events of 1916–23. The Irish state began in an armed rising, won its freedom in a guerrilla war and came into existence during a civil war. The first of these, the Easter Rising of 1916, was a major turning-point in Irish history, of great practical and symbolic importance. It was the culmination of earlier developments.

In the years before the outbreak of war in 1914 it had become clear that potentially dangerous developments were taking place in both parts of Ireland, North and South. The war and its consequences were very significant indeed in the revival of extreme Nationalism in Ireland and the growth of extreme Unionism in Ulster. Politics, instead of dividing on ideological lines – Conservative versus Liberal or Labour – were polarizing on the issue of the Union of Ireland with Britain.

The same period saw the revival of revolutionary Nationalism. There were deep divisions within the Irish Nationalist movement in 1914, a situation made worse by increasing frustration at the slowness of progress towards even a limited form of Home Rule. The IPP, Sinn Féin, the IRB, the Socialist Citizen Army, the Gaelic movement and a host of small groups and organizations competed for the allegiance of Irish patriots. There was also considerable overlap between the memberships of various groups. A significant development was the increasing militarization of Irish Nationalism, with the establishment of a number of paramilitary organizations in imitation of the Ulster Volunteer Force. These included the Citizen Army and the Volunteers. The Citizen Army was an attempt to combine Nationalism and socialism. Certainly conditions for the rise of socialism were ideal in Ireland: Dublin had hideous slums, there was heavy unemployment, pay levels were very low, infant mortality was high and there was a high death rate among adults, for example, from tuberculosis. The early years of the twentieth century saw the rise of an organized trade union movement under James Larkin. In 1909 the Irish Transport and General Workers' Union was set up, with Larkin as leader and James Connolly as deputy leader. In 1911 the *Irish Worker* newspaper was established. From the first, Connolly, a regular and prolific contributor to the paper, tried to combine socialism and nationalism, arguing that the workers would be free and obtain justice only in an Irish national state.

The bulk of the Nationalist movement remained hostile to these aspirations. The great majority of the Nationalist leaders were farmers, small businessmen and middle-class professionals, who preferred to blame the dreadful conditions in Dublin on English rule rather than on the evils of capitalism. Hostility to socialism among the small-farmer class was very deep. The First World War produced an agrarian boom, and Irish farmers were doing well. The role of the Catholic Church was also important; it was very hostile to socialism. Redmond, Sinn Féin and even the Irish TUC believed that capitalism was essential to make Ireland strong. In 1913 came the Dublin lock-out. This arose from a transport strike, and during its course 25,000 workers who refused to give an undertaking not to join a trade union were locked out by their employers, who were organized by leaders of the IPP. It lasted six months, until the workers' resistance collapsed in February 1914.

The Dublin lock-out helped to push Connolly towards a physical-force solution. In November 1913 Connolly and Larkin set up the Irish Citizen Army in Dublin, a well-organized, paramilitary workers' defence corps of about 200 men with the starry plough flag. Its stated aim, apart from defending workers against attack by the police and employers' bully-boys, was to fight for a free and socialist Irish republic.

The Irish Volunteer Force also was established in November 1913. Nominally to defend Ireland against foreign enemies, it was in reality an answer to the UVF: if Unionists were ready to fight to resist Home Rule, Nationalists must show themselves ready to fight to win it. It was quickly infiltrated by the IRB, which formed a small inner command group behind the scenes. These activities were unknown to the respectable front men, such as its nominal leader, the historian Eoin MacNeill, who intended to use the Volunteers to back the constitutional IPP. The physical-force party was becoming stronger all the time after the old IRB activist Tom Clarke was ordered by Clan na Gael in 1907 to return to Dublin from the USA to reorganize the IRB. Clarke's tobacconist's shop became the organizing centre for the

Brotherhood, which quickly attracted a new and energetic leadership. By 1916 it had 2,000 members, who formed a tightly-knit sub-organization within the 180,000-strong membership of the Volunteers. The IRB wished to establish a sovereign republic by force, and its inner leadership claimed to be the legitimate government of the Irish Republic which, as yet, existed only in theory. When, in June 1914, Redmond insisted on taking over leadership of the Volunteers, the IRB became even more closed and secretive. Constitutional and physical-force Nationalism were now as one. In July 1914 guns bought in Germany with money raised by Roger Casement, a distinguished retired civil servant and a sympathizer with the Irish cause, were smuggled into Howth, near Dublin. On their entry into Dublin, the Volunteers clashed with the police and troops, and three people were killed. In general, however, the government adopted a policy of ignoring Volunteer activities, the same attitude as it took to the UVF in the North.

On 20 September 1914 Redmond, in an ill-considered speech at Woodenbridge, committed the Volunteer Force to join the British army, abandoning earlier plans for the northern and southern Volunteers to act as a home defence force. The bulk, some 100,000 National Volunteers, remained with Redmond and the constitutional Nationalists, but about 11,000 men formed the breakaway Irish Volunteers and co-operated with the Citizen Army, for example, in persuading men not to enlist in the British forces. In spite of this, tens of thousands of National Volunteers joined the British army, which made it easier for the IRB conspirators to build up support among those who chose not to volunteer. In August or September 1914 a small group in the IRB leadership decided to launch an armed rising. This led eventually to the Easter Rising of 1916.

In May 1915 a secret IRB military council was set up to organize the rising; it consisted of the IRB activists Tom Clarke, Sean MacDiarmada and Eamon Ceannt, and Patrick Pearse, a teacher and Irish language enthusiast. Roger Casement was active in collecting money in the USA and, in Germany, trying to raise an Irish Brigade for German service from among Irish POWs. He had no success in the latter enterprise. Joseph Mary Plunkett, Casement's assistant and director of operations of the Volunteers, though fatally ill, was also a member of the military council. Connolly joined in January 1916, and the last to join in April 1916 was Tom MacDonagh, a poet and Irish language enthusiast. These men, all republicans but a strange mixture of poets, mystics and practical revolutionaries, were responsible for the Rising.

This rising was planned for Easter 1916 to coincide with a German landing in Ireland. In the event, the Germans backed out but attempted to unload weapons near Tralee between 21 and 24 April 1916. Casement was landed from a U-boat to stop the rising, which was seen as premature, but he was arrested. The British had broken the German naval codes and knew from these, and from sources in Ireland, that the rising was being planned. The Chief Secretary, Birrell, believed the physical-force Nationalists were a tiny minority and was afraid to take firm action in case it precipitated violence. When it became clear that the Germans were involved, the government was ready to act and planned to arrest the leaders on Easter Saturday, 22 April. Eoin MacNeill also tried to stop the rising: orders were sent to cancel the Volunteer manoeuvres planned to cover the beginning of the rising. The small groups dominated by the IRB ignored this order and on 24 April the rising began in Dublin. About 1,500 Nationalist fighters were involved. They seized the General Post Office and other strong points in the city and declared an Irish republic. [**DOCUMENT IV**] The seven leaders, who signed the proclamation, now called themselves the commanders of the Irish Republican Army (IRA).

The rising was over by Saturday, 29 April. It did not spread beyond Dublin, and there were only a few isolated incidents outside the city. The traditional view, that it aroused almost universal outrage in Ireland because it resulted in some 3,000 casualties and caused massive damage in Dublin, is now challenged by those who argue that in fact it is very difficult to judge exactly what Irish public opinion was in 1916, in part because of censorship of the press. Whatever the case, the British threw away any advantage the rising might have given them. Martial law was declared and the military authorities, under the command of Sir John Maxwell, without consulting London began to execute the leaders of the rising after courts martial. This was understandable under the circumstances – a group of terrorists had launched an armed insurrection against the government while that government was engaged in a major war – but it was politically very short-sighted. In all, fifteen men were executed, fourteen in Dublin and one in Cork. The executions were spaced over several days in spite of frantic efforts by political leaders in Dublin and London to stop them. Roger Casement was later hanged in August 1916 after the government publicized his diaries exposing his homosexuality in order to blacken his otherwise excellent reputation. The government was eventually able to bring the executions to an end, but by then the damage had been done. About 1,900 Nationalists were interned in Britain; the majority were released and back in Ireland before the end of 1916. In spite of numerous arrests, the government was unable to eliminate the IRB.

The executions caused massive revulsion in Ireland and began a process which some historians have described as a Catholic political revolution. It completed the emergence of a new politically active middle-class leadership for Irish Nationalism which was overwhelmingly Catholic and made up of small businessmen and members of the lower intelligentsia, such as school teachers and students. The upper middle-class Gaelic enthusiasts, who had made a bid for leadership earlier, were elbowed aside. Sinn Féin, previously a marginal movement among the Nationalist organizations, emerged rapidly as the main beneficiary of the rising, though in the process it was itself transformed.

The rising re-created a strong alliance between Nationalism and the Catholic Church. The act of self-sacrifice of the leaders of the rising was very appealing to Catholic thinking, leading some to write of 'the magic of the dead'. The dead of 1916 came to be seen as Catholic martyrs. The writings of Patrick Pearse, a mixture of nationalism and religious mysticism, were published after his execution and added to this glorification of death. Pearse believed in the need for each generation to make a blood sacrifice to redeem the Irish nation in imitation of Christ's sacrifice on the cross. Bloodshed was, for him, 'a cleansing and sanctifying thing'. Even the socialist Connolly was an active Catholic; he knew that an overt anti-Church stance would alienate the mass of the workers. He wrote in the newspaper *The Worker's Republic* in February 1916 of the need for 'the red tide of war' to flow on Irish soil: without the shedding of blood there could be no redemption. He also expressed the belief that Ireland had betrayed itself by sending its young men to fight in England's war in 1914. An immediate result of the publication of such views after the rising was that thousands of young priests flocked to join Sinn Féin. The funeral of Thomas Ashe, the president of the IRB, who died on hunger strike in September 1916, was attended by the Archbishop of Dublin and hundreds of clergy, high and low. There were more deaths on hunger strike in October 1920, and the funerals again produced fanatical religious demonstrations.

As a result, Irish Nationalism remained rooted in Catholicism. It did not become a force for economic and social modernization, and it did not progress to the stage of emancipatory or democratic nationalism. The Irish state which eventually emerged was to be characterized by an essentially conservative nationalism, dominated by the Catholic hierarchy in alliance with the dominant economic class of small farmers. There *were* progressive forces in Ireland but they were marginal.

The British government continued to make matters worse by its clumsy and inconsistent behaviour. The main beneficiaries were Sinn Féin and the extreme Nationalists. The Easter Rising was habitually referred to as a Sinn Féin rising by government agents though, in fact, the party had nothing to do with it.

Other developments speeded up the growth of Sinn Féin. There was an anti-conscription crisis in early 1918. In April the government, motivated exclusively by the demands of the war, published a Military Service Bill, giving it powers to introduce conscription in Ireland. During the war only 6.1 per cent of the male population of Ireland volunteered for the forces, compared with the between 21 and 24 per cent who volunteered or were conscripted in the other three countries of the Union. A much greater proportion volunteered in Ulster than in other parts of Ireland. This bill was a gift to the Nationalists, who portrayed it as an attempt by Britain to use the flower of Irish manhood as cannon fodder in its war. Again the Catholic clergy became heavily involved in the anti-conscription campaign organized by Sinn Féin. In a series of by-election campaigns, in which Sinn Féin candidates trounced the now discredited IPP, the clergy worked for Sinn Féin. **[DOCUMENTS V and VI]** The Church continued to speak out against British repression, but much less vigorously against IRA violence. In Ulster, Sinn Féin allowed the Church to distribute parliamentary seats between them and the IPP to avoid splitting the Nationalist vote. This, of course, horrified the Unionists, who saw the clergy putting forward pan-Papist candidates as further evidence of 'Rome Rule'.

The rising and the conscription crisis added to the determination of the Ulster Unionists not to be ruled by traitors, who had stabbed the government in the back in collusion with its foreign enemies. If the Easter Rising sanctified the Nationalist cause, the Battle of the Somme in 1916 did the same for Unionists, who made their blood sacrifice when the Ulster Division went over the top and suffered heavy losses. A legend quickly developed that they had worn Orange sashes during the attack. This led to a deepening of hostility between Nationalists and Unionists.

The events of 1916–18 not only changed the Nationalist Irish view of Britain but also the British view of Ireland. It gave urgency to attempts to find a solution to the Irish problem before the end of the war, as many realized that delay would only strengthen the extremists. The wartime coalition government opened the door to compromise between the Unionists and the Liberals, and this made possible a more serious attempt to solve the problem. On 25 May 1916 Asquith announced to the Commons a new initiative on the Irish question. Acceptance of the principle of the exclusion of Ulster made it easier for the British government to settle with the Irish Nationalists while keeping the Ulster Unionists happy. After 1916 it was widely accepted that partition, short-term or long-term, was the only realistic basis on which the Irish question could be settled. Only the Southern Unionists did not share this view. Many of them feared partition because it would leave them isolated. They also feared anarchy and saw a need to co-operate with Redmond's moderate Nationalists to avoid the Nationalist movement's falling into extreme hands, as had happened in the rising. One Southern Unionist, the Earl of Desart, in a memorandum to the Cabinet in November 1919, stated that partition would be 'fatal to Ireland and its prosperity . . . would create a running sore and a perpetual bitterness between north and south . . . To my mind nothing could be more disastrous to both islands than this.' Such views were not listened to.

4.   The Partition of Ireland

After the Easter Rising the Prime Minister, Asquith, tried to implement the 1914 Home Rule Bill before the end of the war. In May 1915 a coalition government, including the Unionists with Carson as Attorney-General, was installed. In June 1916 Asquith handed over conduct of the Irish question to Lloyd George, the Secretary of State for War, with a commission to negotiate a rapid settlement with Redmond, who was equally keen to avoid further evaporation of his party's support.

Many believed that the presence of a Celt in the Cabinet would foster the Irish cause. In reality Celtic solidarity played little part in Lloyd George's thinking. There was no link in his mind between Welsh and Irish Nationalism, and he did not see them as the same. His attitude to Irish Nationalism was always ambivalent: he admired Davitt's agrarian socialism – his rural Welsh background gave him an instinctive understanding of tenant–landlord hostility – but he mistrusted the powerful Catholic element in Irish Nationalism. For Lloyd George, like the Unionists, 'Rome Rule' was a real threat. He opposed the creation of a Catholic national university for Ireland.

Political calculation also played a part: Lloyd George opposed Parnell and Home Rule out of fear that the issue would split the Liberal Party. By 1914 a number of changes in his priorities had taken place. As he aged, he became increasingly keen on the British Empire. Although he had won notoriety as a pro-Boer during the South African War, he wanted the Boer republics to join the Empire, and it was unthinkable to him that Ireland should leave it. Although, after the outbreak of war in 1914, he was loud with calls for the protection of the 'five-foot-five nations' like Belgium and Serbia, he clearly did not include Ireland in that category.

Lloyd George had a deep commitment to social reform as the first task of the Liberal Party. He hoped to make his name as a great statesman by extending democracy in Britain and achieving European conciliation. During the pre-war Home Rule crisis he had already become accepted as an important spokesman on Irish affairs and, though the Irish question was never among his major long-term objectives, he believed that Ireland was an issue on which he could increase his standing. After 1916 his chances of success in Ireland seemed good. By tacit agreement, the Southern Unionists were abandoned, the Conservatives were prepared to compromise, and the acceptance of the principle of exclusion seemed to have satisfied the Ulster Unionists.

High hopes of an easy solution were not fulfilled. When, in September 1914, the government gave a promise to introduce an amending bill to cater for Ulster before the Irish Home Rule Act came into operation, it was not clear whether the exclusion of Ulster from Home Rule was to be permanent or what exactly Ulster would consist of. In an attempt to clarify these points, Lloyd George held separate discussions with the IPP and the Unionists. He failed to find agreement and aroused justified suspicions of duplicity; Lloyd George was trying to obfuscate the whole issue of Ulster's exclusion in order to obtain a quick settlement. From the beginning he assured the Unionists that six Ulster counties would be given a permanent opt-out; at the same time he assured the Irish Party that this was a temporary arrangement. On 10 June 1916 Redmond announced that Lloyd George had offered immediate Home Rule under the 1914 Act, subject to the exclusion of Ulster for the duration of the war. This was a means of sweetening the planned introduction of conscription. On 11 July, Lord Lansdowne in the House of Lords made a contradictory statement that the exclusion of Ulster would be 'permanent and enduring' and that, in the mean time, order would be maintained in Ireland by the application of the sweeping powers allowed to the government under the Defence of the Realm Act. The Unionists were able to sabotage the initiative because the Liberals were afraid they would leave the government. When, on 22 July, Lloyd George told Redmond that Ulster would indeed be given a permanent opt-out, Redmond broke off all negotiations, complaining of a breach of faith. Redmond was later wrongly blamed for the loss of Ulster. This led to a deep mistrust of Lloyd George by the Irish Nationalists. In Ireland the credibility of the IPP was further undermined and the transfer of support to the more extreme Nationalists accelerated.

In December 1916 Lloyd George became Prime Minister after Asquith's indecisive behaviour undermined his own standing. Following complaints about Asquith's handling of the war, Lloyd George and Bonar Law presented him with an ultimatum demanding the creation of a small War Cabinet including Carson. Asquith agreed but later changed his mind. There was a period of confusion, during which the Unionists withdrew their support from Asquith and launched a campaign against him in the press. When leading Liberals refused to back Asquith, he resigned, and Lloyd George formed a new government. The Liberal Party split. Carson became First Lord of the Admiralty and later joined the War Cabinet in July 1917. While Asquith's coalition government had been dominated by Liberals, Lloyd George's was dominated by Conservatives, who were ready to back him because of his support for the Empire and his vigour and energy. Lloyd George was also dependent on the Conservatives because, effectively, he had no party behind him; the majority of the Liberals went with Asquith and voted for him as party leader. The Liberal Party never recovered from this split. The Conservative Party was held together behind the new government by Bonar Law.

From this point, the Irish question became a pawn of British domestic politics. No one had any new ideas. In March 1917 Lloyd George again offered Redmond Home Rule without Ulster. The offer was rejected. The last hope of a compromise settlement came in May 1917 when meetings of the Irish Convention began in Trinity College, Dublin. As a sweetener to the Nationalists, the government released the last of those detained after the Easter Rising, which guaranteed an immediate transfusion of new blood for Sinn Féin. The Convention was merely window-dressing designed to placate American opinion. Sympathy for the Irish cause had long been strong in the USA, where there was a widely held view that America had a duty to help oppressed nationalities and to fight against imperialism. The Irish vote was also a significant political factor in some states. American opinion was the main reason why the government did not dare to use all-out repression against the Nationalists. The Convention was a total flop: Sinn Féin refused to attend, and the Unionists insisted on the exclusion of Ulster from the authority of a Dublin parliament.

By 1918 Lloyd George was even more opposed to Irish Nationalism as the war deepened his imperialist convictions. At this time the Prime Minister seemed to be receiving very poor advice on Irish affairs. Proposals before the end of the war to make Home Rule dependent on the introduction of conscription in Ireland and the imposition of martial law outside Ulster had a disastrous effect on Nationalist opinion, causing a further strengthening of Sinn Féin. In November 1918 the government announced that Home Rule under the 1914 Act would be postponed 'until the condition of Ireland makes it possible', a vague provision which added to the frustration of the

Nationalists. On other occasions it was said that the Act would come into force at the termination of hostilities, by which the government understood the signing of a peace treaty. Lloyd George's main aims were to carry out a programme of social reconstruction in Britain and to achieve a lasting European settlement. Ireland was low among his priorities, as was clear from the low calibre of the ministers appointed to Irish posts. His hostility to Irish Nationalism grew. He blamed Irish agitators for the rash of labour troubles which afflicted Britain after the war, such as the Liverpool police strike. The year 1919 saw more strikes than ever before.

In the 'coupon election' of December 1918 the wartime coalition government came back with a large majority, but Lloyd George had to keep his Conservative partners happy, though they were no longer so opposed to Home Rule. In January 1918 Carson resigned from the government when it became clear that the Prime Minister was still thinking in terms of Home Rule for Ireland as a whole, even if in the long term. In March and April 1918 the Conservative Central Office consulted party opinion on the Irish question and found general approval of Home Rule, provided Ulster was safeguarded. The election had shown that the party no longer felt obliged to play the Orange card to win votes.

On 8 March 1918 Redmond died. The disappearance of the dominant figure of constitutional Nationalism opened the door to a new generation of Nationalist leaders of a very different kind. The most notable were Michael Collins and Éamon de Valera of Sinn Féin. They symbolized the take-over of the Nationalist movement by republicans, the heirs of 1916. In the general election of December 1918, Sinn Féin, standing on an abstentionist manifesto and deliberately appealing to the tradition of Easter 1916, won seventy-three Irish seats; the IPP won six and the Unionists twenty-six. This was, in reality, a rejection of the IPP rather than an endorsement of Sinn Féin by the voters. The new leader of the IPP, John Dillon, was defeated in East Mayo by de Valera, who was in prison during the campaign. Indeed, most of the Sinn Féin MPs elected were in gaol or had fled into hiding as the government had clamped down on republicans in May and June on the pretext that another German plot to help the Nationalists had been discovered. This shabby device was probably thought up by Austen Chamberlain and Walter Long, the latter First Lord of the Admiralty and a strong Unionist. It was typical of the rather aimless policy of the government. Sinn Féin was banned. De Valera, its president, was arrested in May 1918 but escaped from Lincoln gaol in February 1919. After the election, the Sinn Féiners, claiming an overwhelming mandate from Nationalist

Ireland, refused to take their seats at Westminster and instead, in January 1919, set themselves up as the first Irish Parliament, Dáil Éireann, and issued a declaration of independence.

On 21 January 1919 the Dáil established a provisional government of the Irish Republic with de Valera as president, Michael Collins as finance minister and Cathal Brugha (formerly Charles Burgess) as defence minister. Brugha was the nominal head of the Irish Republican Army (as the Irish Volunteers were renamed), the 'army' of the Republic declared at Easter 1916. The key figure was Collins, for de Valera, after his escape from prison, was often away, engaged primarily in raising money in America. Collins was a long-standing leading member of the IRB; de Valera and Brugha were not. De Valera was always suspicious of the role played by a secret society in the emerging Irish state but he needed Collins's organizational skills. The Supreme Council of the IRB retained its role as a small, tightly-knit republican élite, separate from Sinn Féin and the IRA but prominent in the leadership of both. Already in the early days of the provisional government, personal divisions were beginning to cut across the old constitutional/republican division, a factor which was to acquire political significance in the future Irish state. By April 1919 de Valera was president of the Dáil, the IRA and Sinn Féin. In June 1919 he went to the USA, where he raised $5 million for the Irish cause. He was away until January 1921. He left Arthur Griffith as his deputy and acting president of the Dáil, and Brugha as acting president of the IRA.

During his absence, the conflict known variously as the Anglo-Irish war, the Irish war of independence and the Tan War, which broke out in January 1919, was fought. It lasted until 1921. Although called a war, it was in fact a series of guerrilla attacks by IRA irregulars, organized by Collins and the IRB, on the police and British troops. It began with an ambush of members of the Royal Irish Constabulary at Solaheadbeg, and thereafter any servant of the Crown was considered a legitimate target. The majority of the Dáil were against violence, but the extreme wing of the Nationalist movement was able to take the initiative and no one could stop it. The government responded to Nationalist violence with a ban on all Nationalist organizations except the Gaelic League. Dáil politicians tried to contain the violence, but Collins and the IRB encouraged it. Collins revived a classic strategy: he used violence in order to provoke the British into repressive acts, which won recruits for the Nationalist cause, and to revolt British public opinion and so put pressure on the government.

Later, in March 1921, the Dáil was to ratify the earlier actions of the IRA, but from the outset the relationship between them was odd. The IRA saw itself as the legal army of the all-Ireland republic, which had been proclaimed at Easter 1916 but had not yet been achieved. The Dáil government was therefore provisional, and the IRA in the mean time recognized the authority of its army council as superior to that of the Dáil, though its members swore an oath to defend the Dáil against all enemies, foreign and domestic. This subtle point was to become very significant during the Irish Civil War and subsequently.

The 'war of independence' involved about 3,000 IRA fighters against 60,000 troops and 15,000 armed police. Terrorism against members of the RIC and their families led to massive resignations from the force. In March 1920 the first Police Auxiliaries arrived, and later the separate Auxiliary Police Divisions were formed. They were recruited mainly from among ex-soldiers and officers who did not want to return to civilian life, and not, as Irish Nationalist myth would have it, from British prisons. Both units became known from the colour of their uniforms as Black and Tans, and they quickly acquired a very unpleasant reputation because of their methods. One reason was that normal judicial processes to deal with the Nationalists were impossible as juries were systematically terrorized. The police, troops and auxiliaries therefore deliberately used reprisals, such as the burning of villages in which the IRA had operated. This produced a sharp escalation of violence. There were certain key points in this process. In October 1920 the mayor of Cork, Terence MacSwiney, died on hunger strike in Brixton prison. On 21 November 1920, Bloody Sunday, twelve plain-clothes policemen and intelligence officers were murdered by Collins's agents in Dublin. In reprisal, the Auxiliaries fired indiscriminately on the crowd attending an Irish football match at Croke Park, Dublin. Another reprisal was the deliberate burning of the centre of Cork, after which the Auxiliaries wore burned corks on their hats. It is estimated that there were over 1,500 deaths in the war. Many on the Nationalist side were so horrified by the violence that they were ready for a compromise, and Collins became increasingly afraid of splits in the movement. When de Valera returned to Ireland he was not arrested.

Throughout the 'war of independence', steps leading to the installation of a Home Rule government had continued. Under American and Dominion pressure, the government agreed that the 1914 Act should come into force when the last peace treaty was ratified. Unfortunately, it was clear by then that the 1914 Act was no longer acceptable

because of Ulster. A majority even in the Conservative Party wanted
a solution to the long-festering Irish problem. In addition, many
expected Sinn Féin to reject any compromise proposal, and for some
the main function of the exercise was only to improve Britain's image
abroad. In October 1919 a Cabinet committee under Walter Long
was established to make recommendations on the Irish question. It
reported on 4 November 1919 to the effect that Home Rule was
essential to peace in Ireland and should be introduced, provided
Ulster and the unity of the Empire were safeguarded. An Irish
republic was unacceptable and there could be no single Home Rule
parliament for the whole of Ireland. Instead the committee proposed
the creation of two Home Rule governments and two parliaments with
limited domestic powers. Northern Ireland was to consist of the nine
Ulster counties. There would be a Council of Ireland drawn from the
two parliaments to discuss common problems. This would provide an
all-Ireland dimension and could be the core of a future reunion of the
two Irelands. The Act which resulted from these recommendations also
provided that, when a single Irish parliament emerged, it would settle
outstanding questions of finance and customs duties in negotiation
with the British government. The latter clearly regarded the partition
as a temporary expedient but the Act gave the Unionists a cast-iron
guarantee: the reunification of the two Irelands would take place only
when the Northern Ireland parliament agreed to it.

This scheme was designed primarily to solve the Ulster problem,
which it did to the satisfaction of most Tories, but not the Irish
question. In reality it was never intended to do that, though partition,
by shelving the Ulster problem, made possible a British disengagement
from Ireland, which was the primary objective of the government.
When these provisions were put into effect, the Irish question would
cease to be the direct concern of Westminster, which would deal only
with 'imperial' matters of common concern to Britain and Ireland.
Until the later troubles began in 1968, it was a convention that the
Westminster Parliament never discussed any Northern Ireland issues.
The government's basic aim was to remove British rule entirely from
all Irish domestic affairs in accordance with the principle of national
self-determination enunciated at the Paris peace conference. In future
these would be entirely the concern of the two Irish parliaments. This
solution would also have the virtue of leaving no Irish Nationalists
under British rule.

The Cabinet accepted the proposals on 11 November 1919. The only
change was the reduction of Northern Ireland to six counties on the

insistence of the Unionists. This would ensure that the new state had a large Protestant majority. Of course, this ended the Union. Some Unionists wanted Ulster to remain an intrinsic part of the United Kingdom and believed that Home Rule should be imposed only on those areas which wanted it. This was the view expressed by Carson in a Commons debate on 22 December 1919, but his was a lone voice. The Government of Ireland Act became law on 23 December 1920. [DOCUMENT VII] It created two Home Rule Parliaments but stated explicitly that the ultimate supremacy of the Westminster Parliament was 'unaffected and undiminished over all persons, matters and things in Ireland and every part thereof'.

Although the Dáil rejected the Act, elections under it were held on 19 May 1921 in the South and on 25 May in the North. In the South, Sinn Féin won 124 out of 128 seats unopposed. Four Southern Unionists were elected for Trinity College, Dublin; they met briefly as the Southern Parliament because Sinn Féin boycotted it. The only act of the Parliament was immediately to adjourn itself. In the North forty Unionists and twelve Nationalists were elected. The Nationalists elected in both parts of Ireland formed the Second Dáil of an all-Ireland republic. Simultaneously a parallel Dáil government was being set up in the localities in many parts of Southern Ireland, with a system of law courts, a police force and tax collections, alongside the British institutions. These worked, though there was lavish use of intimidation. In large parts of the country the British government's authority was non-existent. The 'war of independence' continued, with many attacks on houses owned by Unionists, large numbers of which were burned down.

As late as June 1921 Lloyd George still favoured repression and opposed negotiations with the Nationalists, but a military solution had clearly failed. General Nevil Macready, the military commander in Ireland, was very pessimistic about the situation. [DOCUMENT VIII] In reports for the Secretary of State for War, he stated clearly that the suppression of Sinn Féin by force was possible, but it is clear, reading between the lines, that he had serious doubts. At the same time he wrote in a letter to the King, who was already very unhappy about the reprisals policy used by Crown forces, that the suppression of the rebels would entail 'an operation of war more extensive and more bitter than would be acceptable to the judgement and conscience of the British people'. On 22 June 1921 the King opened the Northern Ireland Parliament despite worries about his personal safety. Ministers originally wanted him to give a rather aggressive speech, but he was advised by the South African Prime Minister, General Smuts, to use the opportunity to call for peace in Ireland. In a letter to Lloyd George dated 14 June 1921, Smuts pointed out the severe damage being done to the Empire and Britain's image abroad by events in Ireland. He suggested that the King in his speech should offer Dominion status to Southern Ireland now that the opening of the Belfast Parliament had removed for ever the possibility of the coercion of Ulster into a Home Rule Ireland. The King's speech in Belfast, which called for reconciliation in Ireland, went down well. The King simultaneously pressed Lloyd George to seize the opportunity to settle the Irish problem.

The need for some action became clearer. The coalition government was beginning to look very tired as its problems, foreign and domestic, mounted. Lloyd George's plan to create a new party for himself by the fusion of the coalition Liberals and the Conservatives in the United Reform Party came to nothing. By December 1920 the post-war boom was over and Britain was hit by an economic depression. Unemployment reached 1·3 million by March 1921 and 2 million by June. A sharp fall in the export price of coal and cuts in miners' wages led to a series of miners' strikes. Especially worrying was the threat of a Triple Alliance strike of miners, railway workers and transport workers; there was an ever-present fear of syndicalism and communism, which appeared to be powerful in several European states. The rising power of the Labour Party added to nervousness. There was no consolation in foreign policy: no European settlement had been achieved, American pressure over the Irish question remained strong, and there were problems in several parts of the Empire. The government's only hope for success seemed to lie in Ireland. Early in 1921 Bonar Law and Walter Long, the most extreme Unionists, left the government. Lloyd George was also under mounting pressure from the Left in Britain and from his fellow Welsh Liberals over his Irish policy.

Between June and December 1921, Lloyd George concentrated heavily on the Irish question. In spite of mutual atrocities, gentlemanly relations between the two sides had not disappeared during the 'war of independence'. Through people in the Dublin Castle administration, especially Mr (later Sir) Alfred Cope, the assistant under-secretary, Lloyd George had maintained links with Sinn Féin, and a clear message was coming through that they were ready to talk. As early as April 1921 Lord Derby, in disguise, visited Dublin and had talks with de Valera about a possible truce. In May Sir James Craig, the Prime Minister of

Northern Ireland, drove to Dublin and had two hours of secret talks with de Valera. In July the government offered a truce.

On 24 June the Prime Minister wrote to de Valera and Craig inviting them to London. Craig agreed, and de Valera agreed if the government accepted a truce. Smuts visited Dublin on 5 July and persuaded de Valera not to hold out for the republic as a condition for talks, as this was unacceptable to the British. A formal truce began on 10 July. The government was not defeated by arms in the war, but by British public opinion and American pressure. By July 1921 the IRA was exhausted and critically short of weapons. Collins was reportedly amazed when, in that month, the government offered a truce, since he believed the IRA could not have lasted another three weeks under the pressure of British forces.

From 12 July, de Valera was in London and had meetings with Lloyd George on 14, 15 and 17 July. The Prime Minister assured him that no conditions would attach to the negotiations. Although he had already assured Craig that Ulster was safe, he had no intention of allowing the Ulster issue to hold up a settlement. Mobilizing his formidable charm, Lloyd George quickly established a personal ascendancy over de Valera. On 20 July, after a Cabinet meeting, he gave him a document setting out the British terms. Southern Ireland was to enjoy much wider freedom than under the 1914 Act and was to receive Dominion status like Canada, with control of finances and taxation, justice, the police and defence, though there were to be limitations on the size of the Irish armed forces. Britain was to retain the right to use facilities on Irish soil for the British air force and the Royal Navy. Ireland was to impose no tariffs against British imports. Ireland was to recognize Northern Ireland and accept that its rights could not be abrogated except with the consent of the Belfast Parliament.

On 21 July de Valera rejected the draft and demanded the immediate union of North and South. Counter-proposals put forward on 11 August were rejected by Lloyd George. On 16 August the Dáil met in the Dublin Mansion House and swore an oath to maintain the Irish Republic. On the 25th it unanimously rejected the British offer. On 7 September a British note, much toned down at the King's suggestion, offered a conference without preconditions. After a procedural haggle over whether or not de Valera was the representative of a sovereign state, this offer was accepted by the Irish side on 12 September.

The negotiations proper began in London on 11 October and lasted until 6 December. There were five Irish delegates under Griffith and Collins. The British side was represented by Lloyd George,

Lord Birkenhead, Winston Churchill, Hamar Greenwood, the Chief
Secretary for Ireland, and Austen Chamberlain. De Valera stayed in
Dublin, and there has been much speculation about his reasons for
doing so. Probably he knew that a compromise would have to be
reached and that he would be needed in Dublin to hold the Nationalist
movement together when this happened. He expected the delegates in
London to refer any agreement back to Dublin anyway.

In the negotiations Lloyd George used all his virtuosity, mixing
threats and blandishments and holding informal talks with individuals
as a means of dividing the delegates. His secretary and fellow Welshman,
Thomas Jones, also played a major part as a go-between, using Celtic
solidarity as an argument. Lloyd George won over Griffith with the
promise of a border commission to set the frontier between North and
South 'in accordance with the wishes of the inhabitants, so far as may
be compatible with economic and geographic conditions', hinting that
this would make Northern Ireland unviable. This was, it seems, the
Prime Minister's own idea: it seemed to him an honourable way out
of the Ulster problem. The Conservatives were ready to back this ploy
if Ulster were not coerced. In spite of strict orders from de Valera,
Griffith did not hold out for a republic. Lloyd George played his
most audacious card on 5 December, confronting the Irishmen with
two envelopes, one of which, he said, would restart the war while the
other would mean peace. Which, he asked, did they want him to send?
The whole thing was a bluff, as British public opinion would not have
accepted a resumption of the war and Lloyd George knew it. He badly
needed a success; he was planning to hold an early general election in
which he would portray himself as the great peacemaker.

At 2.30 a.m. on 6 December the articles of agreement were signed by
the Irish delegates without reference back to Dublin. [**DOCUMENT
IX**] They believed their acceptance to be provisional: the Dáil would
have to ratify it. If the Dáil refused and war resumed, the onus would
not be on them. They agreed to the partition of Ireland and the
creation of an Irish Free State as a Dominion under royal sovereignty
with the same rights as other Dominions, a governor-general as in
Canada, and control of foreign policy and defence. Ireland was to
take over a share of the national debt and allow the Royal Navy
the use of three treaty ports and other facilities. The size of the
Irish armed forces was restricted. It was laid down that neither
of the Irish states should infringe religious freedom. A Council of
Ireland containing representatives of the two states, as provided for
in the 1920 Government of Ireland Act, could discuss a whole range

of common concerns, including safeguards for the rights of minorities in Northern Ireland.

In later years Lloyd George saw the Irish settlement of 1921 as a great success, describing it as 'the greatest day in the history of the British Empire'. He believed he had corrected a serious error made in 1886, and he saw himself as the bringer of peace to Ireland. In reality his solution alienated everyone: in Britain the Left and many of his Liberal colleagues were outraged by the government's harsh policies during the 'war of independence'; the Right believed too many concessions had been made to men of violence; the Unionists felt betrayed; the Nationalists, forced to accept flawed independence, were left with the bitter taste of disappointed hopes in their mouths. The Irish treaty was followed by a decline in Lloyd George's standing until his final fall from power in October 1922.

After passionate debates in the Dáil from 14 to 22 December 1921 and from 3 to 7 January 1922, a majority, sixty-four votes to fifty-seven, was reluctantly ready to accept the agreement as the best terms available. The minority under de Valera held out against the oath of allegiance to the Crown, to be sworn by all state servants and members of the Dáil under article 4. It is noteworthy that partition was not the main issue; it was anyway seen as temporary. In June 1922 Michael Collins stated quite explicitly that Ulster could not be won by force but only by persuasion at some point in the future. It is also interesting that de Valera did not hold out for the sovereign republic which had earlier been Sinn Féin's objective. The alternative which he put forward during a secret session of the Dáil on 14 December, Document no. 2 [**DOCUMENT X**], was also designed solely to 'meet the sentiments' of the Ulster Unionists and reconcile them to Home Rule. This was a system of so-called external association for Ireland, under which she would be a member of the Empire but without the oath of allegiance. The British rejected this scheme in 1921 but eventually accepted it *de facto* for Ireland in 1936, and it was later to be adopted as a device to enable republics like India to remain in the British Commonwealth.

When the Dáil accepted the treaty, de Valera resigned. A new provisional government under Michael Collins, a convert to pragmatism, was set up, which remained answerable to the British government until an Irish Free State administration was formally established. In fact the two governments overlapped, for Collins was head of the provisional government and finance minister in the revolutionary Dáil government under Arthur Griffith. The constitution of the IFS was published on 16 June 1922: the king was to be the head of state, there was to be a two-chamber Parliament consisting of a Senate appointed by the Irish government and a lower house elected under proportional representation. The Crown would be represented by a governor-general. This was ratified by the Westminster Parliament in the Irish Free State (Constitution) Act of 1922. [**DOCUMENT XIII**] The Dáil now had no authority until a new assembly was elected under the provisions of the 1920 Government of Ireland Act. The election, held on 16 June 1922, was effectively a referendum on the treaty after attempts to form an electoral pact between the two sides failed. It produced fifty-eight pro-treaty and thirty-six anti-treaty Sinn Féin Teachta Dálas (TDs), as the Irish MPs were known. The Irish Free State government took power formally on 6 December 1922. On 7 December the Northern government announced its intention of remaining separate under the 1920 Act.

This formula lasted until 1932, when the Irish began a series of unilateral changes to the relationship between Britain and Ireland. These were not recognized by the British, and the 1921 treaty remained the basis of the legal status of Irish citizens in the UK until 1949. Under the 1921 treaty Irish citizens were also British citizens. They possessed an automatic right of residence in the UK and all the rights enjoyed by British citizens.

While these events were taking place, Southern Ireland was drifting into civil war. Just as had happened after the French and Russian revolutions, the revolutionary party was beginning to split, partly over issues of principle and policy and partly because of personal antagonisms. A majority of the leadership of the IRB and the IRA accepted the treaty, but many of their members did not. Increased hostility to the treaty was caused by an outbreak of serious violence in the North. The IRA, armed by Collins, launched an attack on the institutions of the Northern state, including the invasion and occupation of some border villages. From March 1922 elements in the IRA began to break away from the tenuous control of the provisional government. They portrayed themselves as the lawful army of a sovereign republic proclaimed at Easter 1916, which Collins's government had betrayed. [**DOCUMENT XII**] As the British forces evacuated barracks and other installations in preparation for the Irish take-over, there were often skirmishes between pro- and anti-treaty IRA units simultaneously trying to occupy them. On 22 June IRA members murdered Sir Henry Wilson in London and a unit occupied the Four Courts building in Dublin, from which it defied the government. The Free State government borrowed artillery from the British, who insisted on firm action, and on 28 June they opened fire on the Four Courts. This is taken as the opening of the Irish Civil War.

In Dublin the Civil War was a replay of Easter 1916. Elsewhere it was rather like the Anglo-Irish war, with guerrillas, flying columns, ambushes and atrocities on both sides. The Irish provisional government was forced to use the same methods as the British in the 'war of independence', including the reprisal shooting of prisoners. In the course of it, in August 1922, Michael Collins was killed. After the death of Collins, William Cosgrave became head of the IFS government. By early May 1923 the war was over. In October over 11,000 anti-treaty irregulars were still interned. The anti-treaty forces, significantly, did not surrender but 'dumped' their arms, that is, hid them until they were needed again. [**DOCUMENT XIV**] Peace was totally restored by early 1924. The legacy of bitterness left by the war has affected Irish politics ever since. Physical-force Nationalism, though defeated and cheated of its all-Ireland republic in 1923, continued in existence throughout the following years and remained opposed to constitutionalism.

The boundary commission agreed under the treaty sat during 1924–5 to determine the boundary between Northern Ireland and the Irish Free State. From the outset, it was clear that the representatives of the two Irish states had very different views as to its functions. Fisher from the North wanted no more than tinkering with the border to straighten it and remove enclaves. Eoin MacNeill, now the Southern education minister, wanted a complete redrawing on the basis of local option, which would have taken Fermanagh, Tyrone, parts of Londonderry, South Armagh and South Down into the IFS. After some wrangling, on 7 November the neutral chairman, a South African judge, resigned, followed by MacNeill. In December the two governments came to an agreement to leave the border where it was and still is. The Irish government agreed to scrap the Council of Ireland, in return for which it was excused further payments towards the UK national debt. There was vague talk about future meetings of North and South to settle common problems. The failure of the boundary commission meant that the partition was, for the foreseeable future, permanent.

5.   The Deepening of Partition

The two Irish states began life with the best of intentions. Both had liberal pluralistic constitutions and both intended to cater for the minority communities they contained, Nationalists in the North and Unionists in the South. Both, especially the North, quickly drifted away from these tolerant beginnings. These changes were symbolized in both states by constitutional amendments, which were particularly significant in the South. As a result, during the inter-war years the two Irelands drifted further apart and partition deepened.

The national or border question remained the dominant issue in the politics of both states. The events of the years 1916–23 coloured the politics of Southern Ireland until the 1970s. Politicians' credentials depended not on ideological principles but on what they, or their forefathers, had done during the Civil War, a war which left a legacy of instability and hatred to poison Irish life for two generations. It proved very difficult to break out of this fossilized and narrow 'tribal' political model. The incomplete achievement of national freedom left the country frozen in the national liberation phase of development, apparently incapable of proceeding to social and economic modernization. The origins of the state in the Easter Rising and two wars also left a legacy of militarism. Violence in the national cause was glorified in the ceremonials of the state and in the version of Irish history taught in Irish schools. The national anthem of the Irish Free State is called 'The Soldier's Song'. The IRA continued to regard itself as a state within a state. The Fianna Fáil (Soldiers of Destiny) Party remembered as martyrs the seventy-seven republicans executed during the Civil War by the Free State government. Fine Gael (Tribe of Gaels) members looked on Michael Collins and the other Free Staters killed in the war as its dead heroes. In Northern Ireland the siege mentality of the Unionists persisted, and it presented the image of a fortress armed against its enemies, internal and external.

The political system in both Irish states was subject to corruption, operating on the basis of a spoils system rather than of principle.

Politics for many of its practitioners was a means of exploiting power for group and personal advantage, and political skulduggery was deeply entrenched. A peculiarity of the two states was the abiding weakness of the Left. Socialist parties existed in both but they were marginal. The Irish Labour Party rarely achieved the support of more than 10 per cent of the electorate and the Northern Ireland Labour Party, at its most successful, won only four seats. By convention, British political parties, including the Labour Party, did not organize in Northern Ireland.

The Irish Free State

The inter-war period in the Irish Free State was dominated by Éamon de Valera (1882–1975), the leading figure in Irish politics between 1916 and 1973. In 1926 he emerged from a brief retirement from active politics to establish a new party, Fianna Fáil, the Republican Party. The bulk of the IRA went with him into conventional politics, though a small intransigent group remained outside, committed to the violent struggle. There are still very divided opinions on de Valera in Ireland, depending on the politics of those making the judgement: he is seen as a wise and selfless leader by his own party, Fianna Fáil, but as a scheming murderer by descendants of his Civil War opponents, Fine Gael, and as a double-dealing time-server by the IRA and Sinn Féin.

The aim of Fianna Fáil was the creation of an all-Ireland republic, the restoration of the Irish language and the achievement of economic autarky. De Valera was concerned primarily to define Ireland as a distinct state and not just a pale copy of Britain. He did not understand economics. Although certainly deeply sincere, he had a great capacity for self-delusion and to the end of his life dreamed of creating a united Gaelic-speaking rural Ireland. He was a prisoner of his own myth. As late as 1943 he was still talking of creating 'a land whose countryside would be bright with cosy homesteads, whose fields and villages would be joyous with sounds of industry, the romping of sturdy children, the contests of athletic youths, the laughter of comely maidens . . .' Under the influence of such half-baked fantasies, the IFS pursued policies which, by emphasizing the Catholic and Gaelic character of Ireland as the only basis of true Irish nationalism, deepened the partition. It was all a total illusion, and de Valera's pursuit of it made it difficult for Ireland to come to terms with the real world.

In the eyes of Ulster Unionists, he came to personify the cultural and religious characteristics which made an Irish state so threatening to them. From the outset IFS governments refused to recognize the reality of the major cultural differences between North and South and, especially after 1932 when de Valera was in power, continued to implement policies which evoked hostility and suspicion in Northern Ireland. At the same time, the remaining links with the UK were weakened, culminating in a new republican constitution, the so-called economic war and Irish neutrality in the Second World War. The continuing role of the IRA as a secret organization committed to physical-force Nationalism was also important in deepening the division of Ireland.

The Irish Free State at its foundation was a conservative, rural, economically and socially backward Catholic state. Its political and social life was dominated by small farmers and the small-town middle class of estate agents, solicitors and small businessmen, who were glad to avoid the heavy taxation which the UK needed to fund a welfare state. Many such people had become supporters of Nationalism as much out of self-interest as of conviction. In the rural areas Sinn Féin was never socially radical because it wanted the support of the farmers and their sons, which it obtained. Most of this support was later transferred to Fianna Fáil. One result was that in the IFS, and the later Republic, farmers enjoyed great political weight and were always privileged in respect of taxation. The small independent farmer was also portrayed in official propaganda as the archetypal Irishman living a genuinely Irish way of life.

There was no influential intelligentsia in the IFS. Education, especially in the universities, was neglected, and Ireland continued to present the image of a backward country to the world. The socially conservative, authoritarian and strongly pro-capitalist Catholic Church laid down rules on behaviour and sought to intervene in government in order to attack modernism. Although the IFS was in theory a secular state, no divorce was allowed. A very strict censorship of books and films was introduced between 1923 and 1926. English influences in particular were seen as dangerous to the traditional virtues of the Irish nation. All artificial birth control methods and literature advocating them were illegal. In 1935 it became a criminal offence to import contraceptives. A very narrow-minded view of sex prevailed. Priests prowled lovers' lanes and cinemas looking for immorality. There were strict controls on dance halls and on imported newspapers and literature. The Kerry 'baby scandal' of the early 1980s suggests that this kind of mentality is still not dead in Ireland. It is not surprising that the Irish marriage was often a dreadful experience. As a legacy of the past, especially the land-hunger due to overpopulation, men in rural areas habitually married late, and there was often a wide age gap between husband and wife.

The first government of the IFS, headed by William Cosgrave, a coalition dominated by Cumann na nGaedheal, the party of the pro-treaty side in the Civil War, was very conservative. It created the apparatus of a state closely modelled on Britain, including constitutional politics, the most beneficial legacy of the Union, the police, the civil service and the legal system. There was nothing distinctively Irish about it, apart from a few name changes; the police, for example, became the civic guard (Garda Síochana). Unlike its predecessors, the RIC, its uniformed members were not normally armed.

Cosgrave tried to prove the Irishness of his government by his cultural policy: from 1922 the state embarked on an enthusiastic campaign to restore the Irish language. This was inevitable, as links between political Nationalism, especially its radical wing, and the Irish Ireland movement had been close since the 1890s. Most of the leaders of the Volunteers and Sinn Féin were more or less enthusiastic supporters of the Gaelic League's language revival campaign, and it was taken for granted that, after independence, practical measures would be introduced. The first Dáil appointed a minister for the Irish language.

Irish, which has a good claim to be the oldest living language in Europe, was in a much more precarious position than, for example, Welsh at the end of the nineteenth century. According to the 1891 census, only about 15 per cent of the population could speak it, and it was widely regarded as a sign of backwardness and lack of culture. As in Wales, many Irish-speaking parents deliberately set out to make their children English-speakers, supposedly for their own good. Early pioneers of language revival, like the Young Irelanders, had little success, but in the 1880s a reaction against the decline began. Success in converting the masses was limited. A small number of enthusiasts in the Gaelic League worked hard to spread the message through local branches, publications and the local and national *feis*, the equivalent of the Welsh eisteddfod. In 1921 25 per cent of National School pupils and approaching 75 per cent in secondary schools were already studying Irish. After 1908 a pass in Irish was required for entry to the National University. More important, the language quickly acquired enormous symbolic importance for Nationalists. Without the cultural and spiritual element which the language represented, national independence would be a matter only of jobbery and materialism.

There was a genuine idealism in the ambition to give back to ordinary Irish men and women the cultural heritage which, it was said, had been stolen from them. It was only in the language that genuine Irishness resided; it was the lifeblood of the nation, and without it the Irish would be no more than West Britons. The adoption of an alien language symbolized the nation's slavery. In addition, the Irish language would act as a barrier to all the corrupting influences of the English, the *Gall*, and would enable the Irish people to achieve a higher way of life. Many language enthusiasts were convinced that, throughout the time of English domination, a pure or real Ireland had survived, hidden and uncontaminated, among the Irish-speakers of the remote west, and that this could now be recovered to wipe away centuries of national humiliation.

Fired by the enthusiasm of Gaelic Leaguers, the government after 1922 introduced a range of language restoration policies. Compulsory education was introduced and Irish became an obligatory subject in state schools. It also became an essential qualification for a wide range of jobs in the public service. It appeared on signs and in public documents. It became an official language of the IFS alongside English, and the new ruling class was encouraged to use it in order to restore the social status which the language had lost since the seventeenth century. Lavish state support was given to all things Gaelic, for example, in music, theatre, publishing and broadcasting. There was a sharp decline in Gaelic League membership after 1924, since many believed the state would continue its work. Some members sincerely believed that, within a generation or two, Irish would replace English as the language of the people.

The enterprise was spectacularly unsuccessful. Sean O'Casey described the language revival campaign as 'a fancy fraud and a gigantic sham', while Brendan Behan, an Irish-speaker, mocked the bilingual street- and place-name signs which sprouted all over the IFS. One cause of the failure lay in the fact that the Irish government was a pioneer and had little practical experience of language planning to draw on. Many of the 'experts' who advised the government had an over-simple view of the task which faced them, and too often unfocused enthusiasm rather than a realistic assessment of what was possible prevailed. Difficult problems, such as the development of a standardized Irish to replace the different forms which had evolved, were not faced with sufficient urgency. Also, the language question quickly became confused with other issues. When educationists, teachers or parents expressed reservations or tried to modify language policies, they usually met a bigoted and authoritarian response from government, and their views were dismissed as a product of inadequate religious or nationalist zeal. This was the fate of the Language Freedom Movement set up in 1966 to press for Irish to become an optional subject in schools.

Basically, too much was attempted too quickly, and the limited resources available, in money, teachers, books and so on, were spread too thinly and not concentrated in specific areas or on specific groups. Ireland was a poor country, and it was easier for politicians to pay lip-service to the survival of Irish than to make the hard financial decisions which were needed to make proper provision for it. Public apathy was massive and real motivation hard to create: most Irish children studied Irish but did not learn it, and a completely bogus system developed, for example, to enable pupils to achieve the compulsory pass in Irish needed for the leaving certificate or to show the 'knowledge' of the language needed by a wide range of employees, such as civil servants, bus conductors and postmen. From soon after independence the Irish Free State began to live a gigantic national lie, namely, that Irish had been successfully restored; this persisted until changes in language policy in the 1970s.

The cultural and linguistic policies of the Irish government strengthened Northern Protestants in their determination not to join a state which was becoming visibly less British. The policies also deepened their contempt for an Irish state which seemed ready to sacrifice educational standards in pursuit of the illusion of Gaelic culture.

Other factors deepened the gulf between North and South. Irish governments suffered constant trouble from a small revolutionary wing of the IRA, which after 1923 was moving towards Marxism. In 1924 there was a mutiny of IRB men in the Irish army. In July 1927, after the assassination of the Minister of Justice, Kevin O'Higgins, who had made himself a marked man by his tough actions against the irregulars in the Civil War, the government passed a severe Public Safety Act, equipping itself with sweeping powers to control the extreme republicans, and an Electoral Amendment Act to force Fianna Fáil to give up its boycott of the Dáil or forfeit its seats. This was the first serious move away from what was originally a very liberal constitution, and the first sign of a tough attitude towards civil rights shown by successive Irish governments when their authority was threatened. This was another important legacy of the Civil War, during which the Free State authorities had made lavish use of military courts against the irregulars. From 1924 de Valera and his followers, the losing side in the

Civil War, stood for election to the Dáil but refused to take their seats, as this involved an oath to the Crown. After the passage of the Electoral Amendment Act, de Valera and his fellow Fianna Fáil deputies, forced to play a full role in Free State politics, took the oath to the Crown and their seats in August 1927. This left only a tiny extremist wing of the republican movement that was not prepared to accept partition as a fact for the time being. It was responsible for periodic acts of violence against the Irish state and its agents.

In addition, the Irish economy was very weak in the 1920s and 1930s. One historian, J. J. Lee, has attributed its abysmal performance to the narrowness and lack of enterprise produced by a 'stunted and static society, where self-deception reigns on a heroic scale'. Nationalists continued to blame England, which had neglected Ireland and left a culture of economic dependency, but in reality the Irish were the managers of their own economy, and their performance was poor. Some major works, like the Shannon hydroelectric scheme and the projects of the Electricity Supply Board, achieved spectacular successes, but the overall economic picture remained bleak. High unemployment and high emigration remained characteristic of Ireland after 1922 as they had done previously. As before, Ireland lost the most enterprising of each generation to other countries, and many who stayed became dependent on money sent from Britain and the USA. After independence Ireland remained totally dependent on the UK economically, and became even more so as the USA retreated into Protectionism and placed sharp restrictions on immigration in the 1920s. There was no real improvement of the dreadful conditions in the Dublin slums. The Dáil passed the so-called Democratic Programme in January 1919 as a sop to the Irish Labour Party, including a promise of social reform, but there was to be absolutely no Marxism or socialism, another sign of the influence of the Church and the farming lobby. The power of organized farmers was very strong, and that of organized labour very weak. When, for example, a minimum working conditions law was passed in the late 1930s, agricultural labourers were specifically excluded from its provisions. Ireland was hard hit by the Depression after 1929, which led to the fall of Cosgrave's government.

In March 1932 de Valera came in as Prime Minister (now called by the Gaelic word for leader, *Taoiseach*), a significant change of title from the earlier President of the Executive Committee. He was head of a Fianna Fáil/Labour coalition, which won an overall majority in the Dáil in the 1933 election. De Valera was not just a front for the IRA, as some had feared, and in certain spheres he showed himself pragmatic and increasingly interventionist. Sinn Féin had moved somewhat to the Left under the influence of a new organization, Saor Éire (Free Ireland), a socialist alliance of workers and small farmers devoted to the conservation of the Irish language and the creation of a welfare state, 'the overthrow in Ireland of British imperialism and its ally capitalism'. This injected a bitter 'ideological' element into Irish politics in the 1930s when Cosgrave launched a Red Scare campaign against Fianna Fáil, which quickly saw the folly of its dalliance with the Left. Saor Éire was strongly attacked by the Church as sinful and irreligious, and was actually banned by Cosgrave's government in October 1931, one month after its formation. Fianna Fáil's radicalism was in reality a form of populism and was only a device to win electoral support. Fianna Fáil habitually portrayed its opponents as the party of the wealthy: in reply to Cosgrave's Red Scare tactics, de Valera spread the story that the Cumann was entirely run by freemasons. Irish Free State political life was no more noted for its high intellectual tone than was that of Northern Ireland.

De Valera was very conservative indeed in his social attitudes and pursued a policy of making anti-British republican gestures. For example, he tried to end Ireland's economic dependence on the UK, leading to the so-called economic war of the 1930s. This began with the unilateral ending of repayments to Britain of the land purchase loans made before 1923. This led to retaliatory tariffs against Irish imports and Irish tariffs against British imports. The economic war forced the government to intervene more actively in the economy with measures to encourage arable farming and industry. As a result, Ireland developed manufacturing in footwear, leather, glass, paper, cement, sugar, metal and bricks. There was also a large road-building programme and slum-clearance works which tempered unemployment; but, on balance, Ireland's economy suffered as a result of the economic war. Emigration opportunities fell sharply as a result of the world recession, and Ireland lost British markets for her agricultural exports. Between 1931 and 1938 Irish national income fell by 3 per cent while that of Britain grew by 27 per cent. In 1931 the Irish average income was 61 per cent of that of the British; by 1938 it had fallen to 49 per cent. In the same period agricultural exports fell by more than 50 per cent, and manufactured goods by 33 per cent. When emigration opportunities revived, there was a massive outflow of people, especially when the British wartime economy produced an increased demand for labour. The economic war was ended by agreement in 1938. Britain gave up the three treaty ports of Cobh, Lough Swilley and Berehaven, a major concession to Ireland to try to win her friendship, especially as the European situation was becoming threatening. All this was portrayed by de Valera as a great political victory: he was able to blame Ireland's economic sufferings on British oppression. The end of the treaty ports left Irish neutrality totally uncompromised and, incidentally, made Northern Ireland strategically more vital to the UK.

De Valera also sought to demonstrate Ireland's freedom by his foreign policy. It was a vital symbol of Ireland's nationhood that her voice was heard in international forums. He secured the Irish Free State's admission to the League of Nations in September 1923. De Valera acted as Minister of Foreign Affairs in his first government and was elected President of the League Council in 1932. He strongly supported the work of the League and especially its defence of the rights of small nations.

De Valera carried through major constitutional changes after the 1931 Statute of Westminster loosened residual British powers over the Dominions. In 1933 he announced that Ireland was to be a republic *de facto*. In 1936 he took advantage of Edward VIII's abdication to carry through further changes. The Senate was abolished and the governor-general was stripped of all his powers. Irish citizens were deprived of their British citizenship and British citizens lost their rights in Ireland, though the British ignored the first part of this and continued to regard Irishmen as British, if they wished to be. The right of legal appeal to the Privy Council was also abolished. On 1 May 1937 a completely new constitution was promulgated, [**DOCUMENT XV**] which was thoroughly republican though it did not use the actual word. The name of the state was officially changed to Éire. Ireland now had external association with the Commonwealth and claimed authority over the whole island of Ireland, while recognizing that its legislative power was temporarily restricted to twenty-six counties. Irish was declared the first official language of the state. Under this constitution, power belonged to a two-chamber Dáil, the lower house elected by proportional representation and the Senate, which had delaying powers, partly elected and partly nominated by the Prime Minister and various corporations.

The constitution embodied the principle of the separation of Church and state but obliged the state to abide by Catholic moral teachings in its legislation. Article 44 recognized the special position of the Roman Catholic Church (this article was removed in 1977 after a referendum). Another provision was that various civic rights guaranteed in the constitution, such as freedom of religion, assembly and expression, were 'subject to public order and morality', the latter of course interpreted in a Catholic spirit. Article 41 guaranteed the sanctity of the family, laying upon the state a duty to ensure that mothers were not forced to work and restating the ban on divorce. Divorces obtained outside Ireland were invalid, which had serious implications for property rights and rights over children, for example.

All this was seen by Northern Unionists as proof that Éire was a confessional Catholic state but, as 92 per cent of the population of Southern Ireland were Catholic and it was one of the most observant societies in Europe with a large and influential clergy, there was no real objection to these provisions. It is interesting that the new constitution was passed by a minority of the electorate in a referendum, though the large-scale abstention was probably due more to indifference than to opposition. De Valera probably did not include these religious provisions in the constitution purely out of deference to the Church hierarchy but more as a political move designed to strengthen his own position by pre-empting rivals seeking to use Catholicism to change the basic political system in Ireland in a more authoritarian direction, which he did not totally support. Between the wars there were many signs in Ireland of the influence of corporatist ideas on the Italian fascist model. There was a strong corporatist element in Irish Catholicism, especially after Mussolini's concordat with the Vatican in 1929. As a means of quietening such demands, de Valera in 1938 set up a commission to investigate the possibility of changing Ireland into a corporate state. This sat until 1944, after which its report was shelved.

Divisions among his opponents helped de Valera. Many members of the intransigent IRA went to Spain to fight for the Republic. A temporary threat arose from the fascistic Army Comrades Association or Blueshirt movement under the dismissed Garda police commissioner, General Eoin O'Duffy; it contained many veterans of the Free State army in the Civil War. In 1933 it united with Cumann na nGaedheal to form a new party, Fine Gael, the Tribe of the Gaels. What might have been a danger to democracy in Ireland disappeared when the genuinely fascist wing of the Blueshirts, now calling themselves Greenshirts, went to Spain to fight for Franco. When necessary, de Valera was as ready as Cosgrave to use tough methods against threats to his authority. In June 1936 he banned the IRA after a rash of political murders. This began a period of vicious persecution of the IRA by the Irish government, which was prepared, if necessary, to allow IRA hunger strikers to die. IRA activity had revived in the late 1930s. After a number of attacks on the Irish border, an ultimatum

[**DOCUMENT XVI**] was issued calling for British withdrawal from Northern Ireland, followed by a series of bomb attacks in London and other British cities in the winter of 1938–9 and in the early summer of 1939. Particularly horrifying was an explosion in Coventry, in which women were dismembered by glass flying from shattered shop windows. In June 1939 the Offences against the State Act (Treason Act) introduced internment and trial by military tribunals, methods used by the Free State authorities in the Civil War against de Valera's people, as devices to destroy the IRA. After the outbreak of the Second World War, during the period known in Ireland as the Emergency, de Valera became even tougher, since he was afraid of giving the UK an excuse for breaching Éire's neutrality. The Emergency Powers Act of 1940 allowed the state to intern members of the IRA and to execute them without normal judicial procedures.

About 50,000 Éire citizens volunteered to serve in the UK forces and some 93,000 emigrated to work in Britain during the war, in spite of their country's neutrality. This removed an expensive and potentially dangerous unemployment problem from the country. Neutrality in the war was, for de Valera, a final demonstration of Ireland's independence and sovereignty, and he refused to compromise it, though his country remained economically dependent on Britain for shipping, for the supply of fuel, raw materials and manufactured goods and as a market for Irish products. The policy of neutrality, supposedly justified by the partition, was supported by all political parties and by the great majority of the population.

In June 1940 Neville Chamberlain proposed to hand over Northern Ireland to the Free State at the end of the war if it would come into the war on Britain's side or, alternatively, to make adjustments to the border if it would allow the British navy the use of Irish ports and deal with the German fifth columnists who were believed to be operating in great numbers in Ireland. [**DOCUMENT XVII**] Faced with the U-boat threat to its shipping, Britain was desperate for the Irish bases and could have taken them by force, but it perhaps calculated that the cost would have been too great. De Valera refused both offers, perhaps because he believed Germany was going to win the war or because of his deep mistrust of the British. He probably doubted his ability to persuade a majority of his fellow countrymen to accept involvement in the war. Moreover, there was no guarantee that Northern Ireland would accept union with the South without serious resistance, which might have turned into civil war. The Northern Ireland government was predictably outraged when it learned of Chamberlain's offer. After

America's entry into the war, Ireland again came under pressure, this time from a state it considered its friend, to join in the war. De Valera refused, but he went as far as he could to help the Allied cause without compromising Éire's neutrality.

During the war Southern Ireland was closer than ever before or since to de Valera's ideal of the aloof, pure Celtic jewel, but Irish neutrality further deepened the partition. It caused great bitterness among Northern Unionists, and was made worse by de Valera's insensitive actions, for example, in giving official condolences on the death of Hitler to the German embassy in Dublin. The war experiences, including the German bombing of Belfast, are said to have forged a distinct Ulster identity shared by both Nationalist and Unionist communities. Whether that is true or not, the war was certainly a further cause of the two Irelands' growing apart.

Irish Nationalists have often in the past had an over-simple view of the partition of Ireland. This attitude is summed up in the use of the belittling epithet 'statelet' to describe Northern Ireland. Their refusal to understand the nature of Northern Unionism has sometimes appeared wilful. Perhaps inevitably, the achievement of national independence, for so long seen as the gateway to all manner of group and personal Utopias, proved disappointing. In the cold dawn of reality, nothing much seemed to change. A few signs in Irish and membership of the League of Nations were no compensation for the poverty and narrowness of life in the Irish Free State. It was easy to blame this on the flawed and incomplete nature of the independence. The high hopes once vested in independence were transferred to the achievement of a 32-county republic. Only then would the long dreamed-of perfect world be achieved. The belief that, if the British ended their 'occupation' of Northern Ireland, partition would end is particularly simplistic. In fact, the problem with Northern Ireland was too little British domination in the years 1922–69 (and too much British domination since). Of course, the Northern Unionist view of the South has often been just as distorted and simple-minded, ignoring the large measure of natural unity between the two parts of Ireland and the increasing similarity between them as Anglo-American culture has swept both.

Northern Ireland

Northern Ireland did not suffer a civil war when it came into existence, but serious troubles attended its birth. It was the state no one wanted;

the Unionists, who wanted the Union to be maintained intact, had a large measure of Home Rule forced on them against their will. The first Prime Minister, James Craig, described this as 'the supreme sacrifice in the interests of peace'. The Nationalists in the North rejected the whole thing from the outset. The provisional government in the South imposed a boycott on all goods from the North. There were major sectarian troubles between 1920 and 1922, with the IRA active in many parts of Ulster and Protestant attacks on Nationalists. When George V opened the Northern Ireland Parliament in June 1921, there was serious rioting in Belfast in which some 300 people were killed and £3 million worth of damage was done. In January and March 1922 Craig and Collins came to agreements to bring these troubles to an end. These agreements, especially the second, were surprisingly tolerant documents. [**DOCUMENT XI**] For example, they contained provisions for a mixed Catholic and Protestant police force and regular meetings of representatives of the two communities. All Catholics dismissed from their jobs in the North were to be reinstated and most political prisoners released. Each side would do everything possible to bring violence to an end. There was even talk of a further meeting to discuss the possibility of uniting the two states. All this eventually came to nothing as extreme Unionists sabotaged it and Collins was unable to stop IRA actions against Northern Ireland.

Northern Ireland was made up of six of the nine Ulster counties. Cavan, Monaghan and Donegal were left out for military reasons – it was thought easier to defend the six counties – and because in a nine-county Ulster Roman Catholics would make up almost half the population. The population of Ulster in 1926 was 1·25 million, of whom about 60 per cent were Protestant and 40 per cent Catholic. The relative percentages are still more or less the same today in a population of one and a half million. The Northern Ireland Parliament contained fifty-two seats and, to give Nationalists fair representation, it was initially elected under a proportional system. As in the South, these early generous impulses were quickly abandoned. In 1929 the constitution was revised and PR was abandoned, mainly because Craig believed it threatened to split the Unionist vote. It had already been abolished for local elections in 1922. In the first election in 1921, forty Unionists were elected, and between 1929 and 1968 the Unionists never held fewer than thirty-four seats. There was also a Senate of twenty-four elected by the lower house, together with the mayors of Belfast and Londonderry.

Apart from matters like foreign policy, defence and tax rates, which were determined by Westminster, and certain functions reserved for an eventual all-Ireland parliament, the Northern Ireland government was responsible for all internal matters, including most aspects of finance and social welfare and, specifically, law and order. In June 1922 the Royal Ulster Constabulary was set up, an armed police living in barracks, with three sets of Special Constables: A, full-time officers on six-month contracts; B, armed part-time policemen; and C, a special emergency reserve drawn largely from the Ulster Volunteer Force. By mid-1922 there were over 50,000 full- and part-time police. The A and C reserves were disbanded in the 1930s but 9,000 B Specials remained, all Protestant. The B Specials quickly gained an unpleasant reputation for violence. The Act which established the state laid down that at least one-third of the police force was to be Catholic, but this figure was never reached. At its greatest, Catholic membership was no more than 20 per cent. Catholics were also under-represented in the Northern Ireland civil service, though this was partly their own fault and was not due entirely to a policy of deliberately excluding Catholics.

From the outset, Nationalists saw Northern Ireland as temporary and illegitimate, and refused to have anything to do with its institutions. This was reinforced by powerful community and family pressures. They were also encouraged in these views by Southern governments. The Unionists distinguished between 'Loyal Ireland' (themselves) and 'Disloyal Ireland' (the Nationalists). The word 'disloyalists' was habitually used in Unionist politicians' speeches as was the claim: 'They want the half-crown but not the crown.' It was not surprising that Unionists saw all Catholics as potentially disloyal. These attitudes led one commentator to write of the *Herrenvolk* [master race] mentality' of some Unionists, an almost racial contempt for the Catholic Irish.

The siege mentality of the Unionists remained very strong and it was reinforced by IRA attacks and the Irish Free State's constitutional claims to exercise authority over Northern Ireland. The 1937 constitution, with its special position for the Roman Catholic Church and loosening of ties with Britain, increased Unionist fears. The 1922 Special Powers Act gave the Northern Ireland Minister of Home Affairs wide powers of arrest and detention. Under it the police had undefined power to act against anything which, in their view, was 'calculated to be prejudicial to the preservation of the peace or the maintenance of order'. This was made permanent in 1933 and remained in force until 1972. Police methods in Catholic areas were peremptory and heavy-handed, and punishments for breaches of the Act were severe, including flogging and imprisonment.

Unionist fears were also increased by the fact that Northern Ireland was inherently unstable. Riots and terrorist acts were frequent. The situation was made worse by attitudes in both communities, as neither favoured integration with the other. Discrimination in all forms provided ammunition for extremists on both sides. Unionists indulged in regular manifestations of triumphalism and provocative behaviour, such as Orange parades, which rubbed the Catholics' noses in their inferior position, the Flags and Emblems Act, which made it a crime to show the Irish flag or Nationalist symbols in public, and an official ban on Gaelic names. There was discrimination in jobs and housing. Unemployment in Northern Ireland was endemic and high and, in the competition for work, political factors played a large part: Protestants employed Protestants. Particularly striking was the anti-Catholic employment policies operated by some of the province's largest employers, such as the Harland and Wolff shipyard and the Shorts aircraft factory. Social discontent, already bitter, was made much worse by this. Council housing, on which the majority of the population was dependent, was allocated on political grounds in order to keep the two communities apart and to keep the Catholics together where they could more easily be controlled. This did not mean that Catholics were not housed but that the standards of their housing were often lower. It should be noted that Nationalist local authorities pursued similar policies and had as little interest as the Unionists in bringing about integration. Both communities supported a system of separate education below university level. Even religion seemed to be more extreme, evangelical and intense in Northern Ireland, which experienced many great revivalist movements, Anglican, Presbyterian and Catholic. This contributed to the polarization of the two communities.

Some commentators contrast the discrimination and repression suffered by the Nationalists in Northern Ireland with the privileged position of Unionists in the Free State. There is no doubt that many of the Southern Protestants, or Anglo-Irish as they are sometimes called, continued to enjoy most aspects of their old way of life after independence. They included some of the wealthiest families in the Free State and were prominently represented in the legal and financial professions. In institutions like the Kildare Street Club, the Royal Yacht Club in Dun Laoghaire (they probably continued to call it by its pre-independence name, Kingstown), the Royal Dublin Horse Show, the British Legion, the Orange Order, the Protestant churches, Trinity College, Dublin, and a large number of private schools (in which Irish was usually not taught, though the government paid an annual grant to private schools in which it was, and 'God Save the King' rather than 'The Soldier's Song' was sung as the national anthem) they were able to maintain a separate world. Here those who so wished could live cocooned against the horrors of rule by priests, gunmen and grocers, which is how they saw the Free State. Many, on the other hand, were painlessly assimilated into the life of the community. Of course, it was easy for the Free State authorities to leave the Unionists alone and even to be generous to them, for example, by giving them special representation in the Senate. There were so few of them – they formed about 7½ per cent of the population in 1926, and their relative numbers continued to decline – that they represented no threat to the state. Indeed, in its early years, the main threat to the Irish Free State came from extreme Nationalists, not from Unionists. The great majority of the Anglo-Irish accepted what had happened as irreversible and did not seek to return Southern Ireland to British rule. The Southern Unionist Committee was disbanded after the treaty. Even in the Ulster counties outside Northern Ireland, where there were more substantial concentrations of Protestants, the majority quickly became reconciled to the new order. This was very different from the situation in Northern Ireland, where 40 per cent of the population was made up of Nationalists, most of whom did not accept the state and were apparently working for its destruction, if necessary by violence. The constitution of Northern Ireland did not contain a claim to authority over the South.

Northern Ireland was ruled by Unionist Party governments between 1921 and 1972, when direct rule by Britain came in. There were close and unconcealed links between the Unionists and the Orange Order, and Catholics were not admitted to membership of the party. The politics of Northern Ireland were totally dominated by the issue of the Union, and British political parties were not allowed to operate. The gerrymandering of the boundaries in local government areas and the use of artificial franchises gave the Unionists over-representation in many places. The overall electoral effect can be exaggerated, but it was crucial in some areas, for example, giving the Unionists control of the city of Derry and County Fermanagh, where Protestants were a minority. Northern Ireland was represented in the Westminster Parliament by twelve MPs, each representing a very large constituency, and here too the Unionists were over-represented. In 1981 this was increased to seventeen seats. A one man/one vote electoral system did not come in until 1969, though it must be remembered that this was not introduced in Britain itself until after the election of the Labour government in 1945.

The Northern Ireland political system did not breed the tolerance and willingness to compromise seen in mature functioning democracies. The Unionist leaders were often unattractive characters, manifesting the worst characteristics of the old Ascendancy with few of its redeeming features. James Craig, later Lord Craigavon, was Prime Minister from 1921 to 1940. He became increasingly senile, boasted of his links with the Orange Order and talked of Northern Ireland as a Protestant state for a Protestant people. When, in 1938, de Valera suggested the election of an all-Ireland parliament, he responded with the old Orange motto 'No Surrender'. At a Commonwealth conference he warned the Prime Minister of Australia, Joseph Lyons, to keep a careful eye on his Catholics because 'they breed like bloody rabbits, you know'. Lyons was a Catholic. John Andrews, Prime Minister from 1940 to 1943, stated that, out of thirty-one porters employed in Stormont, the seat of government, only one was a Catholic and he was temporary. Sir Basil Brooke, Lord Brookeborough, Prime Minister from 1943 to 1963, was, at his appointment, regarded as one of a new generation of younger more tolerant Unionists. He still boasted publicly that he had no Catholic workers on his estate, having dismissed them all, and he encouraged other Protestant employers to do the same.

The attitude of the British government towards Northern Ireland was to leave well alone. Although the Westminster Parliament had the power to override decisions of the Northern Ireland Parliament, it never did so. A Speaker's Ruling in 1922 prevented the discussion at Westminster of any matters under the control of the Northern Ireland government. It was clear that the overwhelming desire of the British government was to push a nasty problem under the carpet, a desire shared by the majority of British politicians. An important reason for this was another built-in peculiarity of the Northern state: there was no alternative government to the Unionists, however great their abuse of power. Their numerical dominance was overwhelming, and the majority of Nationalists abstained from any involvement in politics. For example, Nationalist MPs usually refused to take their seats. A few began to sit after 1924, but the boycott ended only in 1965, when the Nationalists took their seats as an official Opposition. As a result of this situation, the British government was never willing to challenge the Unionists in case their government resigned, in which case there would be no one to run Northern Ireland and the whole 'settlement' of the Irish question would be undone. This was in spite of the province's growing financial dependence on the rest of the UK. After 1938 Northern Ireland, which was initially intended to be self-financing from its share of UK taxation, and to make a contribution to the common costs of the whole kingdom, had a constant budget deficit which the rest of the UK was called on to cover. The British government, after a painfully detailed scrutiny of even small items of public expenditure, often paid up without looking too deeply into what the Northern Ireland government was doing, or trying to use its financial control to restrain that government.

When Northern Ireland was set up many people, especially in the South, believed it would be completely unviable economically. In reality, it was richer than the South and had a more balanced economy, with a substantial industrial sector. It certainly had severe economic problems. The province was too dependent on a limited range of economic activities, especially linen, shipbuilding and agriculture. Like the Free State, it was hard hit by the Depression, especially in the shipbuilding industry, though even so the damage was not as devastating as that inflicted on the Irish Free State by the Depression and the economic war with Britain. The North also had a better social security system than the South. That said, its provision of housing, health care and social welfare was inadequate. The Northern Ireland government simply copied British legislation and then looked to Britain to fund it. Subsidies to the province were initially not generous enough to enable it to match the rest of the UK in social welfare. The fact that citizens of Northern Ireland, who were nominally citizens of the UK, were expected to put up with an inferior social welfare system was a cause of constant friction between Belfast and London in the 1920s and early 1930s. Only in 1936 did the British government accept an obligation to pay the costs of giving people in Northern Ireland British social security benefits; full parity did not come until after the Second World War.

The economy of the North was considerably boosted by the war. Agricultural and industrial output expanded substantially and large Allied bases were set up in the province. Substantial sums of capital were brought in, and unemployment all but disappeared. During the war Northern Ireland was of vital strategic and economic importance to Britain, and after 1945 the province was rewarded with a tightening of its links with Britain. From 1946 a series of agreements were signed between the two governments amalgamating the Northern Ireland and British tax, national insurance and welfare systems, which had previously been separate. The British government agreed to help

Northern Ireland to achieve the same standards in education, social welfare and health provision as were being introduced in the rest of the United Kingdom. This brought enormous benefits to Northern Ireland and widened the gap between it and the South in social security.

It is argued by some commentators that since its establishment Northern Ireland has been so much more advanced than the South in terms of social provision and education that it has evolved into a very different society, and that Northern Irish Catholics are different from their co-religionists in the South. The shared war experiences, including terrible German bombing raids on Belfast in April and May 1941, are said to have helped to forge a distinct Ulster identity shared by both communities. Some also argue that the two Irish states were growing together after the war and that the new outbreak of troubles after 1968 ended a period of optimistic developments. This is questionable.

When Éire left the Commonwealth and declared itself a republic in April 1949, the Westminster Parliament passed the Ireland Act guaranteeing that Northern Ireland would remain part of the United Kingdom until the Northern Ireland Parliament decided otherwise. **[DOCUMENTS XVIII and XIX]** Pakenham and a few other Labour politicians tried to persuade the government of the dangers of allowing anti-Catholic discrimination in Northern Ireland to continue, but their views were not heeded. The overriding aim of British politicians was to avoid again becoming involved in the thickets of Irish affairs. Cast-iron guarantees to the Unionists, such as that of 1949, were seen as removing the need to find an acceptable solution to Northern Ireland's basic problems. Devolution did not solve any of these and had only a limited impact on the substantial economic and social differences between the province and the rest of the UK.

6. Overcoming Partition? Ireland since 1949

Southern Ireland began to change after the Second World War. The 1948 general election ousted the Fianna Fáil government and brought to power a new coalition government under John Costello, a strange mixture of conservative Fine Gael, the Labour Party and small parties like Clann na Talmhan (the Family of the Land, a small farmers' party) and Clann na Poblachta (the Family of the Republic), the last a left-wing republican party formed in 1946 by Sean MacBride, son of John MacBride, one of the martyrs of 1916. This growth of small parties was a sign of the lack of ideological divisions in the political system and it was encouraged by proportional representation. It was the rapid growth of Clann na Poblachta which led de Valera to call an early general election in 1948, which he lost. The new government was openly interventionist, as seen in its Long Term Recovery Programme of 1949, and it embarked on large-scale direct investment in economic growth. A trade treaty with the UK in 1948 gave Ireland favourable access to the British market for its agricultural goods. In spite of these measures, the Irish economy remained in difficulty. Rationing, introduced during the Second World War, lasted from 1939 to 1954, longer than in the UK.

The new coalition government also tried to bring in major social reforms. Dr Noel Browne, the Minister of Health, was progressive, but a crisis broke when he tried to introduce a national health service for mothers and children. Most doctors were hostile, and the Church objected, seeing the plan as a threat to the sanctity of the family, which, it said, should be responsible for its members' health rather than the government. Browne resigned in April 1951 when his fellow ministers refused to back him. This was reported in the North as further evidence of the persistence of 'Rome Rule'.

The coalition government split over this and other issues and Fianna Fáil returned to government under de Valera in June 1951. By then the role of the Church in politics was becoming an issue of serious debate in the press and among politicians. There was growing anticlericalism in Fianna Fáil and Church influence fell sharply in the period from 1950 to the 1970s. In the 1960s the censorship laws were relaxed. In 1972 the Republic's constitution was amended to end the special position of the Church. Since then the overt influence of the Church in political matters has declined, though it can still show its teeth as, for example, in a referendum in which a majority rejected proposals to legalize divorce.

Since the 1970s there has also been a much more realistic policy on the Irish language, with less emphasis on compelling people and more on encouraging them to learn and use it. It is difficult to find accurate figures on the language as Irish governments have had a vested interest in concealing the facts. Maps showing areas of the country with over 80 per cent of Irish-speakers in 1961 must be counted among the great works of Irish fiction. In spite of government policies, the *Gaeltacht*, the areas inhabited by native Irish-speakers in the far west and north-west, has shrunk steadily and threatens to wither away completely. The Irish government has, quite rightly, recognized the importance of the *Gaeltacht* as a reservoir of the living language but it has proved difficult to persuade people, especially the young, to stay in linguistic 'reserves' which are often very beautiful but also poor, remote and rural. Attempts to modernize the economy of the areas carry the danger of undermining the very Irishness which the government is so anxious to preserve. The damaging effects of emigration are made worse by another factor, exogamy. As the number of native Irish-speakers shrinks, so it becomes increasingly difficult for one to find another to marry. The chances of the language being successfully transmitted to children in a 'mixed' marriage are limited. It is estimated that there are now only about 30,000 native Irish-speakers, about one per cent of the population. Although a much greater percentage has supposedly learned Irish in school, the great majority of Irish people rarely, if ever, use it. The virtual disappearance of monoglot and native Irish-speakers has serious implications. Now virtually all Irish-speakers are learners, and can only speak it to other learners. The essential artificiality of this situation represents a serious threat to the survival of the language, which, like the Latin of the medieval clergy, is the group jargon of a privileged élite and has little to do with the mass of the people. The days of the Gaelic League have returned; a small minority of enthusiasts foster the language, including strong groups in the Nationalist community in Northern Ireland, while the majority remain indifferent. The Gaelic Athletic Association is the only branch of the Irish Ireland movement which has acquired substantial public support, with games like hurling and Irish football having a large following. The GAA kept its membership ban against the Ulster police and against players and watchers of 'foreign' games like cricket, rugby and association football until 1971.

A government survey on attitudes to the language in 1974 showed that, while a majority of the population were in favour of the survival of Irish, few were personally prepared to go to any trouble to help it survive. There were still enough idiosyncrasies in language policy to give ammunition to the Unionist press in the North. Although Irish ceased to be a compulsory subject on the school-leaving certificate, it counted as two subjects for those who had it.

In the early 1950s the Fianna Fáil government became more interventionist, bringing Ireland into the mainstream of European politics, where social democracy and the social market economy were becoming the norm. It carried through a series of social welfare measures, laying the foundations for a welfare state in the Republic, though it remained inferior to that in the UK, including Northern Ireland. For example, the Health Service introduced in 1973 is available only to people on low incomes; others have the option of taking voluntary health insurance, a class-based system with graded premiums and graded health care provision. There were also improvements in the education system: a major report on education in the Republic, published in 1966, revealed serious deficiencies and led to a number of changes and great improvements. Free secondary education came in 1967. Until recently the Irish education system remained inferior to the British.

Fianna Fáil fell in 1954 after imposing sharp tax increases, which were necessary to finance the welfare measures and continuing government investment in the economy. Costello returned as head of a Fine Gael/Labour government. Fianna Fáil won again in 1957. This illustrates the emergence in Éire of a two-party system, Fianna Fáil and Fine Gael, with a weak Labour Party and sometimes independent MPs holding the balance. Fianna Fáil was traditionally more republican and radical in social terms, while Fine Gael was, until the 1970s, more conservative. The doctrinal differences between the two main parties remain vague.

In spite of continuing economic weakness, social reform continued after the Second World War. The beneficial effects of Marshall Aid and other loans and grants which Éire received, amounting to about £150 million, were becoming clear. There was considerable economic growth under the Fianna Fáil government elected in 1957.

Sean Lemass, long a keen supporter of government intervention to boost the economy, became Prime Minister in 1959 and de Valera became President; he died in 1975. This change in itself marked a major break with the past, though its effects have still not worked themselves out in the Republic. Many people of progressive views argue that de Valera's legacy, especially the 1937 constitution, is still holding the country back. Lemass adopted a policy of concentrating on economic and social modernization, partly in the hope that this would make the prospect of reunification more attractive to Northern Unionists. In the late 1960s there was economic improvement, and for the first time since the Famine of the 1840s, emigration ended and the population increased. Ireland also began to take advantage of its neutrality by adopting a more active role in the United Nations, for example, by providing troops for peace-keeping forces. In this it has continued to break out of its narrow obsession with Britain and Northern Ireland, a process begun by de Valera in the 1930s.

The UK and Ireland joined the EEC together in 1972, in spite of the crisis in Northern Ireland, and since then Ireland has continued to modify its economic dependence on the UK. Effective economic planning (called 'programming' to avoid accusations of socialism) was introduced and there has been large-scale foreign borrowing. The government gave generous encouragement to foreign firms to set up in business, with mixed results. Ireland has proved much more enthusiastically European than has Britain, and the equality it enjoys as a sovereign state in the councils of the European Community has done a great deal to enhance its national self-confidence. It has a very young population, a diversifying economy and a social welfare system which is close to that of Britain.

In the 1980s Ireland began changing very rapidly. The political scene saw the emergence of new parties, the Progressive Democrats and Sinn Féin (The Workers' Party), a genuinely socialist party and the political wing of the Official IRA. Membership of the EEC and of the European Parliament forced the main Irish political parties to define themselves in more conventional European terms, and the two main parties attached themselves to the Christian Democratic and Centrist groups. The 1970s also saw the revival of an organized fundamentalist republican movement in response to events in Northern Ireland, but electoral support for it has remained low. A general election in November 1992 saw a spectacular increase in support for the Labour Party, confirming a development which began with the unexpected election of the party's candidate for the presidency, Mary Robinson.

Fianna Fáil remains the largest party, regularly taking 40 per cent of the vote.

Many old attitudes are dying away, and Ireland is becoming a more secular society. This was marked by significant symbolic changes: in 1979 barrier contraceptives became available on a limited basis, and more freely available since 1985. Average family size has fallen sharply. A controversial High Court decision in 1992, permitting an under-age girl pregnant as the result of a sexual assault to obtain an abortion in Britain, may be a sign that another wall has crumbled. The ban on divorce remains.

There were some signs of the two Irelands growing together in the 1960s. In 1963 Terence O'Neill, the new Prime Minister of Northern Ireland, worried by rising electoral support for the Northern Ireland Labour Party and under some pressure to reform from the British Labour government, sought to give Unionism 'a human face', to build bridges to Catholics in Northern Ireland while at the same time not frightening the Unionists. This was an extremely difficult balancing act. In January 1965 Sean Lemass was invited to visit him in the North, the first time an Irish Prime Minister had visited Northern Ireland. O'Neill later visited Dublin. In 1966 limited ceremonies commemorating the fiftieth anniversary of the Easter Rising were allowed in Northern Ireland, which aroused unfavourable comment from extreme Unionists. After the 1965 general election in Northern Ireland, the Nationalist MPs, led by Eddy McAteer, agreed to take their seats at Stormont and to act as an official Opposition. There was a perceptible movement towards moderation in the Nationalist camp. In 1969 John Hume, later one of the founders of the constitutional Nationalist Social Democratic and Labour Party, defeated McAteer in Derry.

These developments had the dangerous double effect of raising Catholic hopes of improvement without fulfilling them, while at the same time arousing fears among Unionists that a sell-out of Ulster was being contemplated. Ian Paisley emerged as a leader of extreme Unionism, and the Ulster Volunteer Force was revived in 1966, to be declared illegal by O'Neill in the same year after a number of sectarian murders. In spite of the ban, the movement continued its activities. Growing criticism from his colleagues forced O'Neill to resign in April 1969 in an attempt to maintain unity in his party, which was threatening to fall apart and split the Protestant vote, always a frightening prospect for Unionists. By then the renewed bout of Troubles had started.

There is much misunderstanding of the origins of this latter-day Northern Ireland problem. These Troubles did not have their origin in despair caused by economic depression. The Northern Ireland economy boomed in the mid-1970s as a result of government help and successful policies to attract investment, though traditional industries were in trouble and structural unemployment remained stubbornly high. The IRA was also not responsible: the Troubles after 1969 produced the Provisional IRA, not vice versa. Between 1956 and 1962, after Sinn Féin did well in the North in the 1955 general election, the IRA tried to mount a campaign in the North, but this was a complete failure. Internment was employed in both Irish states, and the campaign received little support among Northern Nationalists. This was seen by some as a sign of changing attitudes among Catholics in Northern Ireland. In 1968 the IRA announced its opposition to violence and its conversion to Marxism. From then on, its stated aim was to achieve a socialist electoral victory in both parts of Ireland as the basis for an all-Ireland state.

Conflict began when the Northern Ireland situation became unstable and seemed to be changing. The Nationalist minority, instead of challenging the legitimacy of the Northern state, began to demand equality within it. The traditionally dominant majority saw this as a threat to its status. Serious trouble started with the Northern Ireland Civil Rights Association set up in February 1967 to press for social and electoral reforms in the province, including the abolition of the B Specials and the Special Powers Act, and an end to all forms of discrimination. Although the movement was dominated by Catholics, it did not have as one of its stated aims the end of partition. In October 1968 a small group within the NICRA formed People's Democracy, a revolutionary movement with its strongest following among students. This was quickly infiltrated by extreme Nationalists. Its activities led to a sharp move to extremism among the Unionists and undermined both Catholic and Protestant moderates. After a period of growing civil disorder, the flashpoint came on 4 January 1969, when a civil rights march from Belfast to Derry, organized by People's Democracy, was attacked by a Protestant mob at Burntollet Bridge. On the same day the police ran amok in the Catholic part of Derry, the Bogside, attacking the population indiscriminately. This behaviour was later officially condemned by the report of the Cameron Commission. Television programmes were broadcast in the UK showing conditions in Northern Ireland. This was the first time the people of Britain were able to see exactly what was happening in the province. Previously there had been massive ignorance. In the summer of 1969 there was more serious rioting in Derry and Belfast. As disorder spread, the Northern Ireland government could no longer control the situation and on 14 August it asked for troops to be deployed. The British government announced a programme of major reforms to end discrimination, and in August 1969 the first UK troops arrived.

This was the first direct British involvement in Northern Ireland affairs since 1922. This had the effect of making the new Troubles last much longer than any earlier outbreaks, which were dealt with by the RUC using traditional methods such as intimidation and internment. British involvement prevented the use of these techniques. The IRA, which, after a period of confusion, again became active in late August 1969 to protect Catholic areas in Belfast and Derry against Unionist violence, was more firmly based in Northern Ireland and no longer controlled from the South. In December 1969 the movement split. A small Official IRA remained committed to a Marxist solution, and the majority went into the Provisional IRA. Since then it has used traditional, violent methods in an attempt to achieve a united Ireland. Mistakes by the Northern Ireland and British governments, such as the use of internment by the former in August 1971, ensured support and a steady flow of recruits for the Provisional IRA from the Nationalist community. Unionist paramilitary organizations also became increasingly active.

Northern Ireland came under direct rule from Britain on 24 March 1972, when Brian Faulkner resigned as Prime Minister after the British government refused to give him the wide emergency powers he demanded. Since then there has been a constant search for solutions.

Northern Ireland represents a huge cost to the UK Treasury. In 1965–6 it cost £48 million, in 1979–80 over £1,000 million, and the costs continued to rise. British political culture was traditionally, at least until the advent of Mrs Thatcher as Prime Minister, based on compromise and consensus; the Northern Ireland situation, involving stark polarization, did not fit this tradition. The situation of the early 1990s is eerily reminiscent of that before 1914. Moderate political parties are under constant pressure from extremists. There are one million Unionists, hostile to any compromise which seems to threaten the Union, and some of them are armed and ready to use force. The period from 1974 saw the emergence of extreme Unionist movements, including Vanguard and the Democratic Unionist Party. The main Nationalist party, the Social Democratic and Labour Party, set up in 1970, has been under pressure from the more extreme Provisional

Sinn Féin. The Provisional IRA, although a very small minority of the Nationalist population, has not been deserted by its community. The Alliance Party, a middle-class party which supports the Union and has a substantial Catholic membership, remained marginal in Northern Ireland politics, and so did the Northern Ireland Labour Party.

From the 1980s the Irish Republic, though its politicians continued to make ritual noises about partition, had more important things to worry about than Northern Ireland. It was no longer as ready as in the 1970s to change itself in the hope of removing Unionist fears and making reunification acceptable to them. Irish economists admitted, that Éire would find it difficult to cope with Northern Ireland if it were reunited with the Republic without continued massive economic subventions from someone. Unemployment in Northern Ireland and in the Republic is high. Both have very young populations and both have experienced renewed emigration. The Republic has very high direct and indirect taxation and is a much more expensive place to live than Northern Ireland, though prices there are higher than the UK average. The Irish government is in a difficult position: it is terrified of the Troubles spreading to the South but must not be seen by the people of the Republic as puppets of the British. Fianna Fáil especially has been ready to use the partition issue as political ammunition against Fine Gael. In spite of that, Jack Lynch, Fianna Fáil Prime Minister from 1966 to 1973, brought in a very harsh new Offences against the State Act to control the Provisional IRA, which is regarded as a threat to the Republic as well as to the North. There has been growing co-operation between Ireland and the UK in security matters. In the period 1969–81 there were 2,167 deaths resulting from terrorism, and 23,000 were injured. The casualty figures then declined and the security situation improved, but the security authorities admitted that there was no acceptable military solution to the problem. No society can survive in a permanent state of emergency.

The economic situation was badly affected by the civil disorder. Northern Ireland is further from economic viability than it has ever been. There is very high unemployment, a massive balance of payments deficit and a huge public sector borrowing requirement. Seventy per cent of Northern Ireland's GDP is government spending. The British government formerly had a policy of trying to solve the political problem by throwing money at it; it has not worked. One result is that Northern Ireland has some of the finest leisure facilities in the UK, but attempts to boost employment by giving firms incentives to set up in the province have been less successful.

Direct rule continues under the Northern Ireland Act of 1974, which is annually renewed, as is the 1974 Prevention of Terrorism Act. Attempts have been made to find a political solution based on compromise, usually involving the restoration of devolved powers to a Northern Ireland authority. For example, in November 1973, after elections to a new Assembly, a power-sharing executive was set up, backed by the SDLP, the Alliance and part of the Unionist Party. In December 1973 the Sunningdale Conference was held. At this the Irish government agreed that Northern Ireland should remain part of the UK until a majority there voted otherwise, a Council of Ireland was established and more anti-terrorist co-operation was agreed. The executive was set up on 1 January 1974 with the Unionist Brian Faulkner as head and Gerry Fitt of the SDLP as his deputy. This produced another movement to the extremes among Unionists. In the British general election of February 1974 anti-executive Unionists took eleven out of the twelve Ulster seats. On 14 May 1974 the anti-executive Ulster workers' strike began. The executive collapsed on 29 May as a result of the strike, and direct rule returned. Elections to a Constitutional Convention on 1 May 1975 resulted in a clear victory for extreme Unionist parties. In March 1976, after prolonged attempts to find a compromise between the two sides had failed, the Convention was dissolved. Another compromise attempt, Lord Whitelaw's 'rolling devolution' scheme of 1982, was sabotaged when Sinn Féin and the SDLP refused to take their seats in the Assembly elected in November.

These events showed that a new form of Unionism was emerging under proletarian and lower middle-class leaders, very different from earlier aristocratic leaders like Lord Brookeborough, Terence O'Neill and Robin Chichester-Clark. The Official Ulster Unionist Party tried to keep alive the old-style Unionism, with the object of integrating Northern Ireland in the UK. They have lost support to the Democratic Unionist Party (Paisleyites), which wants the end of direct rule and the restoration of a Stormont government, or even an independent six-county Ulster, as the only safeguard against a sell-out of Ulster by Britain. Paisley is the most popular politician in Northern Ireland. The extreme 'gut Unionism' of small farmers and Belfast workers, which finds expression in the Democratic Unionist Party, is not well understood in Britain. British politicians were bewildered to find that the language of sectarianism heard in the 1880s is still in common use a hundred years later.

There is in Britain a false belief that, if only the extremists on both sides can be eliminated, the moderate majority will find a compromise.

In reality there is no moderate majority when it comes to the basic question of whether Northern Ireland should be part of the UK or of an Irish state. In spite of earlier optimism, cultural convergence and common membership of the European Community, there seems little prospect of North and South growing together. If anything, they have grown further apart. Northern Ireland is very different from the South; even Catholics from the North are different from their Southern co-religionists, largely because of the education system in the North. Some Northern Catholics, seeing major problems in a union between North and South, favour the solution of a self-governing nine-county Ulster, independent of Dublin and London. There is a related movement in the Republic which advocates the devolution of more power from Dublin to the localities.

Northern Ireland is a relic of British imperial rule but, because it is on Britain's and Éire's doorstep, it cannot be shrugged off and abandoned to civil war, as India was. The problem cannot be resolved by altering a line on a map or by allowing one or another group in the North, the Unionists or the Nationalists, to achieve its aspirations. The basic problem is that Northern Ireland is an unworkable political unit. Under present circumstances it is unlikely to be integrated into the British state or into the Irish Republic or given independence, which very few of its inhabitants want anyway. This is illustrated in several plans put forward in an attempt to solve the problem. The 1983 New Ireland Forum in Dublin suggested a condominium, an equal sharing of power over all aspects of government in Northern Ireland by the UK and the Republic. This is unacceptable to the Unionists, and such a joint authority would keep Northern Ireland in a kind of colonial or semi-colonial dependency on the presupposition that it is incapable of self-rule. The IONA (Islands of the North Atlantic) scheme, based on a confederation of Britain, Éire and Northern Ireland, is fanciful and unrealistic, for no Irish government would dream of restoring the Union, even in a symbolic form. The Kilbrandon Report of autumn 1984, the result of an inquiry by a private working party, proposed control over internal affairs in the province by a five-man executive, taking majority decisions and made up of the Northern Ireland Secretary, the Irish Foreign Minister and three members directly elected in the North under a proportional representation system. This executive would be answerable to an Assembly, also elected under PR. Again, there were serious practical objections, and it was not made clear what would happen if the Assembly vetoed the decisions of the executive.

One of the reasons why the Unionists are so frightened of any form of joint sovereignty is a fear that the Nationalists will use it to pressurize the majority into a united Ireland. This is a major weakness of the Anglo-Irish Agreement of 1985. Thus there is a marked lack of progress and direction on the issue in Britain and in both parts of Ireland. Public debate in the Republic about the nature of Irishness remains limited and resembles a shouting match between two sets of extremists over the bewildered heads of the mass of the population. Some talk about a European solution. This is popular with the prosperous and progressive middle class in the Republic, known collectively from the leafy suburbs where many of them live as 'Dublin 4'. It suggests that there are policies available to a European authority which have not been tried by the British government and been seen to fail. It is doubtful if such policies exist. Extreme Unionists already see the EC, a product of the Treaty of *Rome*, as a Papist plot. The claims of 'Dublin 4' to speak for Ireland are, in any case, questionable. They are usually ardent supporters of the 'modernization' of the Republic through, for example, reform of its laws on abortion and divorce. This enables their traditionalist opponents to attack them for undermining the most important element in Irish national identity, religion, in the process doing what the British had done for centuries, portraying the Irish as the victims of a backwardness and insularity from which they can be rescued only by becoming more like the British.

The British government has not succeeded in persuading the Unionists to make a distinction between necessary internal reforms in Northern Ireland, designed to remove discrimination in employment and other fields, and creeping reunification. Even limited involvement of the Irish Republic in Northern affairs is seen by Unionists as the first step in a process leading to a Dublin take-over. The guarantee by the Republic as part of the Anglo-Irish Agreement that there would be no united Ireland without the consent of the Northern majority might concentrate minds in Northern Ireland, but its validity depends on future changes in the politics of the Republic. There is a temptation for Irish politicians to exploit the Northern issue for political purposes. Neil Blaney, after his expulsion from Fianna Fáil in 1971, established Independent Fianna Fáil, which exploited the border issue and gained substantial support in border areas, especially Donegal. The behaviour of the Provisional IRA has done much to lessen the attraction of this approach in recent years.

Arguably, the Anglo-Irish Agreement has made the situation more unstable. Provisional Sinn Féin, which took 11·4 per cent of the vote in the 1987 general election, welcomed it because it promoted mistrust between the British government and the Unionists. Some argue that it encouraged the IRA to increase its violence in the belief that British public opinion would eventually force the government to withdraw. A Sinn Féin leader, Gerry Adams, said in 1991: 'The British always adopt stiff upper lips in these circumstances. There is a long history of them putting up an intransigent front while making arrangements to go.' A poll held in 1973 showed a substantial majority in favour of the Union, including a large number of Catholic voters. A 1989 study, *Ulster: Conflict and Consent*, by Tom Wilson, quoted evidence that a majority of Catholics in the North do not want union with the Republic but rather a position of equality in the North. Yet so far, the British government has made the same mistake as Terence O'Neill in the 1960s: it has raised Unionist fears and done nothing to calm them; and raised Nationalist expectations but done nothing to satisfy them.

There may be other long-term solutions. An integrated education system in Northern Ireland has been talked about since 1970, but little has been done. While both communities support it in theory, they oppose it in practice. Outside the middle class, mixed marriages and socializing between the communities are difficult. Projects, for example by the Churches, to break down barriers receive a great deal of publicity but their real impact is very limited. They may change inter-personal judgements, but not inter-group judgements. For reasons of security people tend to stay in their own narrow communities. It seems that the partition of Ireland will last for many more years.

Illustrative Documents

DOCUMENT I Speech of Charles Stewart Parnell at Ennis, 19 September 1880 (extract)

'. . . I may, perhaps, also be permitted to point out to you a noteworthy feature connected with this meeting, especially as I think it is a sign of the times and a sign of the progress of our movement. When first I addressed you in last July twelvemonth, this square was glittering with the bayonets of police (cheers); and I promised you then, pointing to the force, that if we could build up a determined and united Irish party, in a very few years this military force would be abolished altogether. (Cheers) Today there is not a single constable present at this meeting (cheers) . . . Let us look upon this as a happy omen for the future, as the first recognition in our history by the Government of England of the ability of our people to maintain order for themselves, and consequently to govern themselves (cheers); and let me ask you, fellow-countrymen, in return so to bear yourselves during this meeting and after this meeting as to show that you are worthy of practical power and self-government. (Cheers) . . . The resolution which has been proposed and seconded in such able terms is one inculcating the necessity of union among ourselves and independence of every English Ministry, whether it be Tory or Radical. (Hear.) . . . Depend upon it that the measure of the Land Bill of next session will be the measure of your activity and energy this Winter. (Cheers) It will be the measure of your determination not to pay unjust rents; it will be the measure of your determination to keep a firm grip of your homesteads (cheers); it will be the measure of your determination not to bid for farms from which others have been evicted, and to use the strong force of public opinion to deter any unjust men among yourselves, and there are many such, from bidding for such farms. (Hear, hear) If you refuse to pay unjust rents; if you refuse to take farms from which others have been evicted, the land question must be settled, and settled in a way that will be satisfactory to you. It depends, therefore, upon yourselves, and not upon any commission or any government . . . Now, what are you to do to a tenant who bids for a farm from which another tenant has been evicted? (Several voices: Shoot him!) I think I heard somebody say "Shoot him." (Cheers) I wish to point out to you a very much better way, a more Christian and charitable way, which will give the lost sinner an opportunity of repenting. (Laughter and hear hear!) When a man takes a farm from which another has been evicted you must shun him on the roadside when you meet him; you must shun him in the streets of the town; you must shun him in the shop; you must shun him in the fair green and in the market place, and even in the place of worship. By leaving him severely alone, by putting him into a moral Coventry, by isolating him from the rest of his countrymen as if he were the leper of old, you must show him your detestation of the crime he has committed. If you do this you may depend on it that there will be no man so full of avarice, so lost to shame as to dare the public opinion of all right-thinking men in the country and transgress your unwritten code of laws. (Loud cheers) . . . We have been accused of preaching communistic doctrines when we told the people not to pay an unjust rent, and the following out of this advice in a few of the Irish counties has shown the English Government the necessity for a radical alteration of the land laws. But how would they like it if we told the people some day or other not to pay any rent until this question is settled? (Cheers) . . . I hope it may never be necessary for us to speak in that way. (Hear) I hope the question will be settled peaceably, in a friendly manner and justly to all parties. (Hear) If it should not be settled, we cannot continue to allow this millstone to hang round the neck of our country, throttling its industry and preventing progress. (Cheers) It will be for the consideration of wiser heads than mine whether, if the landlords continue obdurate and refuse all just concessions, we shall not be obliged to tell the people of Ireland to strike against rent until this question has been settled (cheers); and if the 500,000 tenant farmers of Ireland struck against the 10,000 landlords I should like to see where they would get police and soldiers enough to make them pay' (Loud cheers).

(*The Times*, 20 September 1880.)

DOCUMENT II   Report of the Council of the Belfast Chamber of Commerce on the Irish Government Bill, presented and adopted at an extraordinary general meeting of the Chamber, 17 March 1893

We believe that the Economic and Social condition of Ireland renders it singularly unfitted for Home Rule. The population is not homogeneous – it is radically divided on the lines of race and of religion, and the two parties are filled with distrust and with historical jealousy of each other. The chief Economic necessity of the country is the development of manufactures, trade and commerce; but the vast majority of the population have no appreciation of the conditions under which alone such necessities can be met. They do not seem to know that, while a Government can destroy prosperity by destroying security and credit, no Government can create it in the face of insecurity and suspicion.

The resources of Ireland are unequal to supporting a national government. A few figures will make clear what we mean. The total valuation of the country is a trifle over £14,000,000 sterling; while the valuation of Great Britain exceeds £200,000,000. The income tax of Ireland is £556,000; in Great Britain it amounts to £13,296,000. Compare again the main evidences of commercial and trading wealth. The coal raised in Great Britain in 1891 was valued at £74,055,274; that raised in Ireland the same year is given at £44,542. On the railways in Great Britain 306,000,000 tons were carried in 1891; in Ireland 4,410,731 – and of this amount the railways terminating in Belfast carried 41%. The total railway receipts of Ireland (of which 34% is taken by the above-mentioned lines) amount to about 4% of the railway receipts of Great Britain. The capital of all the railways of Ireland is under £40,000,000 – about £10,000,000 less than of the Lancashire and Yorkshire Railway alone. The registered tonnage of the ports of Great Britain is 7,990,261, that of all the ports of Ireland is 256,439, and of this Belfast holds 55%. It is no exaggeration to say that more than one English county is at least as well fitted economically and socially for self government as the Kingdom of Ireland.

Again, the Commercial and Manufacturing districts (which we claim to represent) form but a fraction of the country. The greater part of the rest of Ireland has neither the resources, the capital, nor the unity of race or interest requisite to render it capable of standing alone without the support of Imperial credit. It is manifestly unfitted for a tremendous experiment, and nothing seems to promise that such an experiment would succeed. The first condition for successful trade is security. In Belfast, under the shelter of the Union, protected by British Commercial laws, with the advantage of British Fiscal Legislation in which we share, there has grown up the first great development of trade and industry ever known in the history of the country . . . The development of that trade is entirely dependent on the

maintenance of the sense of security; and it is useless to shut our eyes
to the fact that the mere introduction of the Bill, which we have been
deputed to examine, has seriously shaken credit . . . The depreciation
of values in Irish securities already amounts to over £3,000,000 sterling.
We may add that from no political quarter has any assurance been given
that this Bill, even if passed, will really secure a final settlement of the
Irish question. It would seem therefore that agitation, uncertainty and
consequent insecurity are to be perpetual in Ireland.

We find no provisions in the Bill calculated to allay these growing
apprehensions. There is a complete absence of any real practical
protection from unwise or unjust taxation, or from the unwise or
unfair application of taxation. The safeguards provided we regard
as wholly nominal, and of no practical operative value, and we are
confirmed in this view by finding them – and especially the veto of
the Lord Lieutenant, whether exercised on the advice of his cabinet
or by the express instructions of her Majesty – treated with derision by
the Nationalist press. The provisions as to the electorate of the Second
Chamber are such, that the majority there must necessarily reflect the
views of the Legislative Assembly . . . The representation offered is a
mockery; and we may plainly state the fact that, under the provisions
of the Bill, we are defenceless.

Beyond this, we find that the proposed Irish Legislature, in which we
are invited to appear in a minority of about one-fifth, has no definitely
settled constituencies or electorate. It is proposed to enact that at the
end of six years that body may re-organize itself, and the majority are to
be at liberty to take steps to insure our absolute impotence. There is no
protection offered beyond the vague provision that 'due regard' is to be
had to the population of the constituencies. We submit to the Chamber
that the time for a 'due regard' to the population is now, before the
Bill has been considered in Parliament at all; that the proposition to
perpetuate the over-representation of the Nationalists, which has been
openly admitted by the Prime Minister and by the Chancellor of the
Exchequer, and which cannot be denied, is cruelly unjust; and we
find difficulty in conceiving how any man could support it by his
vote, whatever his politics. We state that such a distinct disregard
of equity in a leading clause of the Bill gives us every reason to
doubt profoundly the justice of any portion of it which even on
the surface may seem fair . . . The effect of these considerations
on the minds of the commercial and manufacturing community is
so serious, that beyond question if the Bill passes into law, large
amounts of capital, and many branches of industrial enterprise, will

migrate to Great Britain, or the United States or the Colonies. The disorganization of industry, and the social disturbances sure to follow the enactment of the measure, will cause intense suffering among the working classes of Ireland, and drive them in large numbers to England and Scotland to compete with their brethren there for employment.

We have given our best attention to the proposed Fiscal arrangements . . . so far as we can understand their meaning, they fill us with grave apprehension. It is in any case impossible that an Irish Legislature, with a temporary arrangement of constituencies, and a system of restraints and vetoes hanging upon it, could start with high credit; and it is the more impossible since some of those certain to be its ministers have publicly associated their names with the principle of the repudiation of contracts . . . We beg to report to you that we consider the fiscal arrangements as altogether unsatisfactory . . . We find also that the *Economist*, writing from the London point of view and with the authority of one of the leading financial papers published, says – 'It is proposed to establish a Legislature in Ireland which will be in chronic want of money.' Even such paper surplus as is shewn is dependent on the contribution of that amount by the British Parliament, namely £500,000 a year, for a limited period of years, towards maintenance of the Irish Police. At the end of that period it is a vanishing quantity, unless the Irish Government have in the meantime cut down the cost of Constabulary by one-third – in our view a most unlikely contingency. There is a complete consensus of opinion on this point, and we repeat our belief that the Bill is not financially sound. We see no margin for error; no provision for a reduction in the amount of the Excise; no provision for possibly diminished yield from Income Tax or Post Office; no provision for the necessary expenses of the working of the Legislature, for the salaries of the Ministers or of the working staff; no provision for pensions to the existing police, for pay for the police of the future, or for the salaries and pensions of new judges and civil servants. It is superfluous to point out that there will be no funds available for the encouragement of technical education, science or art. Such a Government will have difficulties from the outset, and there can be no escape from the necessity of new taxation to supply inevitable deficiencies. Existing capital, in which we are interested, must be subjected to fresh taxes. The savings of the country, the natural source of future capital, must be cut short, and the steady growth which our City has witnessed for generations must be checked . . .

We observe there are no substantial restrictions on Legislation on the subjects of the Poor Law and Education – either could readily be made a means of gross injustice; and we feel justified in pointing out that the public utterances of the Nationalist leaders, and the resolutions passed by public meetings and Boards of Guardians in many parts of Ireland, have shown such disregard, not merely of equity between man and man, but of economic principles, that the thought of important powers being devolved on the representatives of such ideas fills us with consternation . . .

We have asked in vain for any definite statement of social or material improvements to Ireland likely to result from the Bill. The only methods towards such ends suggested by the Nationalists point to Protection and Bounties; and we note that, while the Bill excludes Protective Duties, there is nothing to prevent an extravagant system of Bounties. It is therefore manifest that the majority are to be at liberty to waste taxes raised in Belfast and Ulster, in the attempt to create and foster trades in other places on a false and unnatural foundation. No one can read the Bill, even cursorily, without seeing that in several ways taxation can be applied to crush political opponents. In addition to the Bounty system, we need only instance the income tax, the death duties, the transfer and stamp duties, and the licensing system – any one of which can easily be manipulated, under the Bill, against a hostile minority. We conceive we have a right to say that we cannot rely upon the character of the Nationalist leaders in dealing with commercial interests. Some of these gentlemen defend and advocate the system of Boycotting – a system which the Prime Minister himself states is supported by the sanction of the 'murder which must not be denounced'; they are the men whom he has charged with preaching a doctrine of 'public plunder'. We know them as the authors of the Land League, the doctrines of which the Chancellor of the Exchequer asserts to be the 'doctrines of treason and assassination'. We know that by judicial decision a large number have been convicted of being 'guilty of a criminal conspiracy', and of having been subsidized through their Parliamentary Fund by the sworn enemies of England. These are not mere opinions; they are undeniable facts. We cannot be expected to accept a Bill proposing to place us at the mercy of such men . . .

All our progress has been made under the Union. We were a small insignificant town at the end of the last century, deeply disaffected and hostile to the British Empire. Since the Union, and under equal laws, we have been welded to the Empire, and have made a progress second to none. In 1783 we find the population of Belfast was 13,105;

in 1891 it was 255,590. In 1861 the valuation of the City was £270,930; in 1893, £741,000. In 1837 the funds at command of the three Banks, having Head Offices in Belfast, were £1,488,134; in 1892 the amount was £14,797,285 . . . In 1837 the tonnage of vessels clearing from Belfast was 288,143; in 1892 it was 2,053,637 tons, and the Harbour receipts are 39% of the total Harbour receipts of all Ireland. The Foreign imports are £9,106,000, 36% of the sum total imported into Ireland. The Customs duties paid in Belfast are 44% of the whole collected in the Island. The Customs amount to £2,376,511; Inland Revenue about £900,000 more, making together over £3,250,000, being a contribution to the Imperial Revenue surpassed by no port in the United Kingdom except London and Liverpool; it is nearly a million more than the Prime Minister's estimate of Ireland's share of the Imperial Expenditure.

We wish to emphasize the fact that this progress has been made under PRECISELY THE SAME LAWS AS THOSE WHICH GOVERN THE OTHER CITIES AND PROVINCES OF IRELAND. It is specially noteworthy that the raw material employed in our staple manufactures is chiefly imported. The Iron and Steel for our great Shipyards; two-thirds of the Flax for our Spinning Mills; and the Coal for all industrial and domestic purposes are all imported articles. There is no privilege in this respect that is not open to every other city and town in our island. We earnestly protest against haste in legislation, and especially in legislation which goes to the roots of the Constitution. What Ireland wants is time in which the healing effects of the remedial measures of the Imperial Parliament may bear fruit . . .

We can imagine no conceivable reason – no fault that we have committed – which would justify the treatment which this Bill prepares for us. We are to be driven out of our present close connection with England and Scotland; we are to be deprived of the power to control our own future; and we are to be handed over to the government and guidance of men of whose principles we disapprove and whose capacity has never been applied towards the practical advancement of the material interests of the country.

We are of the opinion that the reasonable wants of Ireland would be fully met by any mode of dealing rapidly and simply with the Land question, consistent with justice and honour; by some arrangement for Local Government similar to that lately created in England and Scotland; by an adequate reform of Private Bill Procedure; and by such aid from Imperial credit as would in a sensible and economic way assist the development of Irish industries, where and when such assistance might be required.

We conclude by restating as broadly, and firmly as possible, our opinion that the circumstances of Ireland – the peculiarities of its population – its poverty and absence of natural resources – render the experiment of autonomy exceptionally dangerous, and we anticipate from such an experiment absolute disaster; that the Bill as drawn is radically and incurably unjust; and that, should it become law, the result would be a blow as deadly to Irish commercial interests as were the measures framed centuries ago intentionally to ruin Irish trade.

The Bill has been avowedly introduced to terminate government by what is called Coercion, but it cannot be enforced in this City or in the Province of Ulster except by Coercion – Coercion by the force of the Empire directed against those who have done most service to Ireland, the most industrious, the most law-abiding, the most faithful and dutiful subjects the Queen has in the whole island.

(Bodleian Library, Oxford, MS Bryce 218, fol. 23.)

DOCUMENT III   Extract from speech of Sir Edward Carson in the House of Commons, 11 February 1914

Ulster looms very largely in this controversy, simply because Ulster has a strong right arm, but there are unionists in the south and west who loath the bill just as much as we Ulster people loath it, whose difficulties are far greater, and who would willingly fight, as Ulster would fight, if they had the numbers. Nobody knows the difficulties of these men better than I do. Why, it was only the other day some of them ventured to put forward as a business proposition that this bill would be financial ruin to their businesses, saying no more, and immediately they were boycotted, and resolutions were passed, and they were told that they ought to understand as Protestants that they ought to be thankful and grateful for being allowed to live in peace among the people who are there. Yes, we can never support a bill which hands these people over to the tender mercies of those who have always been their bitterest enemies. We must go on whatever happens, opposing the bill to the end. That we are entitled to do; that we are bound to do. But I want to speak explicitly about the exclusion of Ulster . . . If the exclusion of Ulster is not shut out, and if at the same time the prime minister says he cannot admit anything contrary to the fundamental principles of the bill, I think it follows that the exclusion of Ulster is not contrary to the fundamental principles of the bill . . .

On the other hand I say this, that your suggestions – no matter what paper safeguards you put, or no matter what other methods you may attempt to surround these safeguards with for the purpose of raising what I call 'your reasonable atmosphere' – if your suggestions try to compel these people to come into a Dublin parliament, I tell you I shall, regardless of personal consequences, go on with these people to the end with their policy of resistance.

(House of Commons Debates, vol. 58, cols. 175–6.)

DOCUMENT IV   The Proclamation of the Irish Republic, 24 April 1916

Poblacht na h-Éireann

The Provisional Government of the Irish Republic to the People of Ireland.

Irishmen and Irishwomen: In the name of God and of the dead generations from which she receives her old tradition of nationhood, Ireland, through us, summons her children to her flag and strikes for her freedom.

Having organized and trained her manhood through her secret revolutionary organization, the Irish Republican Brotherhood, and through her open military organizations, the Irish Volunteers, and the Irish Citizen Army, having patiently perfected her discipline, having resolutely waited for the right moment to reveal itself, she now seizes that moment, and, supported by her exiled children in America and by gallant allies in Europe, but relying in the first on her own strength, she strikes in full confidence of victory.

We declare the right of the people of Ireland to the ownership of Ireland, and to the unfettered control of Irish destinies, to be sovereign and indefeasible. The long usurpation of that right by a foreign people and government has not extinguished the right, nor can it ever be extinguished except by the destruction of the Irish people. In every generation the Irish people have asserted their right to national freedom and sovereignty; six times during the past three hundred years they have asserted it in arms. Standing on that fundamental right and again asserting it in arms in the face of the world, we hereby proclaim the Irish Republic as a sovereign independent state, and we pledge our lives and the lives of our comrades-in-arms to the cause of its freedom, of its welfare, and of its exaltation among the nations.

The Irish Republic is entitled to, and hereby claims, the allegiance of every Irishman and Irishwoman. The Republic guarantees religious and civil liberty, equal rights and equal opportunities to all its citizens, and declares its resolve to pursue the happiness and prosperity of the whole nation and of all its parts, cherishing all the children of the nation equally, and oblivious of the differences carefully fostered by an alien government, which have divided a minority from the majority in the past.

Until our arms have brought the opportune moment for the establishment of a permanent national government, representative of the whole people of Ireland, and elected by the suffrages of all her men and women, the Provisional Government, hereby constituted, will administer the civil and military affairs of the Republic in trust for the people. We place the cause of the Irish Republic under the protection of the Most High God, whose blessing we invoke upon our arms, and we pray that no one who serves the cause will dishonour it by cowardice, inhumanity, or rapine. In this supreme hour the Irish Nation must, by its valour and discipline, and by the readiness of its children to sacrifice themselves for the common good, prove itself worthy of the august destiny to which it is called.

Signed on behalf of the provisional government,

Thomas J. Clarke, Sean Mac Diarmada, Thomas MacDonagh, P. H. Pearse, Eamonn Ceannt, James Connolly, Joseph Plunkett.

(National Museum of Ireland EW2L.)

DOCUMENT V   Election leaflet of Count Plunkett in the North Roscommon by-election campaign, February 1917

WHY YOU SHOULD SUPPORT COUNT PLUNKETT

1. BECAUSE he is an Irishman and a Count of the Holy Roman Empire, the highest honour the Pope could confer on a layman.

2. BECAUSE he is the man who stood shoulder to shoulder with Parnell and Davitt, whose fight against Landlordism left every farmer in Ireland secure in his land.

3. BECAUSE he is the man who was recently insulted by the Royal

Dublin Society – which is formed from the dregs of Landlordism in Ireland – in their blind bigotry and lust for revenge.

4. BECAUSE he is the man who sacrificed his three sons in order that your son, and every Irish father's son, should be saved from the sacrifice.

5. BECAUSE he is an educated man and a consistent Irishman, and will prove a worthy advocate of the wants of his people.

6. BECAUSE he will not associate with the Irishmen who cheered in Parliament when his son was shot against a wall for loving Ireland.

Will you insult him in North Roscommon, as the Royal Dublin Society did and tell the British Government that he is not the man you want?

NO! THERE ARE IRISHMEN IN NORTH ROSCOMMON YET.

(IPD 16 National Library of Ireland poster collection.)

DOCUMENT VI   1918 Sinn Féin Election Manifesto

The coming General Election is fraught with vital possibilities for the future of our nation. Ireland is faced with the question whether this generation wills it that she is to march out into the full sunlight of freedom, or is to remain in the shadow of a base imperialism that has brought and ever will bring in its train naught but evil for our race. Sinn Féin gives Ireland the opportunity of vindicating her honour and pursuing with renewed confidence the path of national salvation by rallying to the flag of the Irish Republic.

Sinn Féin aims at securing the establishment of that Republic

1. By withdrawing the Irish Representation from the British Parliament and by denying the right and opposing the will of the British Government or any other foreign Government to legislate for Ireland.

2. By making use of any and every means available to render impotent the power of England to hold Ireland in subjection by military force or otherwise.

3. *By the establishment of a constituent assembly comprising persons chosen by Irish constituencies as the supreme national authority to speak and act in the name of the Irish people, and to develop Ireland's social, political and industrial life, for the welfare of the whole people of Ireland.*

4. By appealing to the Peace Conference for the establishment of

Ireland as an independent nation. At that conference the future of
the nations of the world will be settled on the principle of government
by consent of the governed. Ireland's claim to the application of that
principle in her favour is not based on any accidental situation arising
from the war. It is older than many if not all of the present belligerents.
It is based on our unbroken tradition of nationhood, on a unity in a
national name which has never been challenged, on our possession of
a distinct national culture and social order, on the moral courage and
dignity of our people in the face of alien aggression, on the fact that
in nearly every generation, and five times within the past 120 years
our people have challenged in arms the right of England to rule this
country. On these incontrovertible facts is based the claim that our
people have beyond question established the right to be accorded all
the power of a free nation.

Sinn Féin stands less for a political party than for the Nation;
it represents the old tradition of nationhood handed on from dead
generations; it stands by the Proclamation of the Provisional Government of Easter, 1916, reasserting the inalienable right of the Irish
Nation to sovereign independence, reaffirming the determination of
the Irish people to achieve it, and guaranteeing within the independent
nation equal rights and equal opportunities to all its citizens. Believing
that the time has arrived when Ireland's voice for the principle of
untrammelled national self-determination should be heard above every
interest of party or class, Sinn Féin will oppose at the polls every
individual candidate who does not accept this principle. The policy
of our opponents stands condemned on any test, whether of principle
or expediency. The right of a nation to sovereign independence rests
upon immutable natural law and cannot be made the subject of a
compromise. Any attempt to barter away the sacred and inviolate
rights of nationhood begins in dishonour and is bound to end in
disaster. The enforced exodus of millions of our people, the decay of
our industrial life, the ever-increasing financial plunder of our country,
the whittling down of the demand for the 'Repeal of the Union', voiced
by the first Irish Leader to plead in the Hall of the Conqueror to
that of Home Rule on the Statute Book, and finally the contemplated
mutilation of our country by partition, are some of the ghastly results
of a policy that leads to national ruin. Those who have endeavoured
to harness the people of Ireland to England's war-chariot, ignoring
the fact that only a freely-elected government in a free Ireland has
power to decide for Ireland the question of peace and war, have
forfeited the right to speak for the Irish people. The Green Flag

turned red in the hands of the Leaders, but that shame is not to be laid at the doors of the Irish people unless they continue a policy of sending their representatives to an alien and hostile assembly, whose powerful influence has been sufficient to destroy the integrity and sap the independence of their representatives. Ireland must repudiate the men who, in a supreme crisis for the nation, attempted to sell her birthright for the vague promises of English Ministers, and who showed their incompetence by failing to have even these promises fulfilled.

The present Irish members of the English Parliament constitute an obstacle to be removed from the path that leads to the Peace Conference. By declaring their will to accept the status of a province instead of boldly taking their stand upon the right of the nation they supply England with the only subterfuge at her disposal for obscuring the issue in the eyes of the world. By their persistent endeavours to induce the young manhood of Ireland to don the uniform of our seven-century-old oppressor, and place their lives at the disposal of the military machine that holds our nation in bondage, they endeavour to barter away and even to use against itself the one great asset still left to our Nation after the havoc of centuries.

Sinn Féin goes to the polls handicapped by all the arts and contrivances that a powerful and unscrupulous enemy can use against us. Conscious of the power of Sinn Féin to secure the freedom of Ireland the British Government would destroy it. Sinn Féin, however, goes to the polls confident that the people of this ancient nation will be true to the old cause and will vote for the men who stand by the principles of Tone, Emmet, Mitchel, Pearse and Connolly, the men who disdain to whine to the enemy for favours, the men who hold that Ireland must be as free as England or Holland, or Switzerland or France, and whose demand is that the only status befitting this ancient realm is the status of a free nation.

ISSUED BY THE STANDING COMMITTEE OF SINN FÉIN.

(IPD 28 National Museum of Ireland EW 129.)

DOCUMENT VII   Government of Ireland Act, 1920

An Act to provide for the better Government of Ireland. 23 December 1920.

Be it enacted by the King's most Excellent Majesty . . . as follows:
ESTABLISHMENT OF PARLIAMENTS FOR SOUTHERN IRELAND AND
NORTHERN IRELAND AND A COUNCIL OF IRELAND.

1. – (1) On and after the appointed day there shall be established for
Southern Ireland a Parliament to be called the Parliament of Southern
Ireland consisting of His Majesty, the Senate of Southern Ireland,
and the House of Commons of Southern Ireland, and there shall
be established for Northern Ireland a Parliament to be called the
Parliament of Northern Ireland consisting of His Majesty, the Senate
of Northern Ireland, and the House of Commons of Northern Ireland.

(2) For the purposes of this Act, Northern Ireland shall consist of
the parliamentary counties of Antrim, Armagh, Down, Fermanagh,
Londonderry and Tyrone, and the parliamentary boroughs of Belfast
and Londonderry, and Southern Ireland shall consist of so much of
Ireland as is not comprised within the said parliamentary counties and
boroughs.

2. – (1) With a view to the eventual establishment of a Parliament for
the whole of Ireland, and to bringing about harmonious action between
the parliaments and governments of Southern Ireland and Northern
Ireland, and to the promotion of mutual intercourse and uniformity in
relation to matters affecting the whole of Ireland, and to providing for
the administration of services which the two parliaments mutually agree
should be administered uniformly throughout the whole of Ireland, or
which by virtue of this Act are to be so administered, there shall be
constituted, as soon as may be after the appointed day, a Council to
be called the Council of Ireland.

(2) Subject as hereinafter provided, the Council of Ireland shall
consist of a person nominated by the Lord Lieutenant acting in
accordance with instructions from His Majesty who shall be President
and forty other persons, of whom seven shall be members of the
Senate of Southern Ireland, thirteen shall be members of the House
of Commons of Southern Ireland, seven shall be members of the Senate
of Northern Ireland, and thirteen shall be members of the House of
Commons of Northern Ireland.

The members of the Council of Ireland shall be elected in each case
by the members of that House of the Parliament of Southern Ireland or
Northern Ireland of which they are members. The election of members
of the Council of Ireland shall be the first business of the Senates and
Houses of Commons of Southern Ireland and Northern Ireland . . .

The President of the Council shall preside at each meeting of the Council at which he is present and shall be entitled to vote in case of an equality of votes, but not otherwise.

The first meeting of the Council shall be held at such time and place as may be appointed by the Lord Lieutenant.

The Council may act notwithstanding a vacancy in their number, and the quorum of the Council shall be fifteen; subject as aforesaid, the Council may regulate their own procedure, including the delegation of powers to committees.

(3) The constitution of the Council of Ireland may from time to time be varied by identical Acts passed by the Parliament of Southern Ireland and the Parliament of Northern Ireland, and the Acts may provide for all or any of the members of the Council of Ireland being elected by parliamentary electors, and determine the constituencies by which the several elective members are to be returned and the number of the members to be returned by the several constituencies and the method of election.

POWER TO ESTABLISH A PARLIAMENT FOR THE WHOLE OF IRELAND

3. – (1) The Parliaments of Southern Ireland and Northern Ireland may, by identical Acts agreed by an absolute majority of members of the House of Commons of each Parliament at the third reading (hereinafter referred to as constituent Acts), establish, in lieu of the Council of Ireland, a Parliament for the whole of Ireland consisting of His Majesty and two Houses (which shall be called and known as the Parliament of Ireland), and may determine the number of members thereof and the manner in which the members are to be appointed or elected, and the constituencies for which the several elective members are to be returned, and the number of members to be returned by the several constituencies, and the method of appointment or election, and the relations of the two Houses to one another; and the date at which the Parliament of Ireland is established is hereinafter referred to as the date of Irish union:

Provided that the Bill for a constituent Act shall not be introduced except upon a resolution passed at a previous meeting of the House in which the Bill is to be introduced.

(2) On the date of Irish union the Council of Ireland shall cease to exist and there shall be transferred to the Parliament and Government of Ireland all powers then exercisable by the Council of Ireland, and (except as far as the constituent Acts otherwise provide) the matters

which under this Act cease to be reserved matters at the date of Irish union, and any other powers for the joint exercise of which by the Parliaments or Governments of Southern and Northern Ireland provision has been made under this Act.

(3) There shall also be transferred to the Parliament and Government of Ireland, except so far as the constituent Acts otherwise provide, all the powers and duties of the Parliaments and Governments of Southern Ireland and Northern Ireland, including all powers as to taxation, and, unless any powers and duties are retained by the Parliaments and Governments of Southern Ireland and Northern Ireland under the constituent Acts, those Parliaments and Governments shall cease to exist:

Provided that, if any powers and duties are so retained the constituent Acts shall make provision with respect to the financial relations between the Exchequers of Southern and Northern Ireland on the one hand and the Irish Exchequer on the other.

(4) If by the constituent Acts any powers and duties are so retained as aforesaid, the Parliaments of Southern Ireland and Northern Ireland may subsequently by identical Acts transfer any of those powers and duties to the Government and Parliament of Ireland, and, in the event of all such powers and duties being so transferred, the Parliaments and Governments of Southern Ireland and Northern Ireland shall cease to exist.

LEGISLATIVE POWERS

4. – (1) Subject to the provisions of this Act, the Parliament of Southern Ireland and the Parliament of Northern Ireland shall respectively have powers to make laws for the peace, order, and good government of Southern Ireland and Northern Ireland with the following limitations, namely, that they shall not have power to make laws except in respect of matters, exclusively relating to the portion of Ireland within their jurisdiction, or some part thereof, and (without prejudice to that general limitation) that they shall not have power to make laws in respect of the following matters in particular, namely:

(1) The Crown and the succession to the Crown, or a regency, or the property of the Crown (including foreshore vested in the Crown), or the Lord Lieutenant, except as respects the exercise of his executive power in relation to Irish services as defined for the purposes of this Act; or

(2) The making of peace or war, or matters arising from a state of

war; or the regulation of the conduct of any portion of His Majesty's subjects during the existence of hostilities between foreign states with which His Majesty is at peace, in relation to those hostilities; or

(3) The navy, the army, the air force, the territorial force, or any other naval, military, or air force, or the defence of the realm, or any other naval, military, or air force matter (including any pensions and allowances payable to persons who have been members of or in respect of service in any such force or their widows or dependants, and provision for the training, education, employment and assistance for the reinstatement in civil life of persons who have ceased to be members of any such force); or

(4) Treaties, or any relations with foreign states, or relations with other parts of His Majesty's dominions, or matters involving the contravention of treaties or agreements with foreign states or any part of His Majesty's dominions, or offences connected with any such treaties or relations, or procedures connected with the extradition of criminals under any treaty, or the return of fugitive offenders from or to any part of His Majesty's dominions; or

(5) Dignities or titles of honour; or

(6) Treason, treason felony, alienage, naturalization, or aliens as such, or domicile; or

(7) Trade with any place out of the part of Ireland within their jurisdiction, except so far as trade may be affected by the exercise of the powers of taxation given to the said Parliaments, or by regulations made for the sole purpose of preventing contagious disease, or by steps taken by means of inquiries or agencies out of the part of Ireland within their jurisdiction for the improvement of the trade of that part or for the protection of traders of that part from fraud; the granting of bounties on the export of goods; quarantine; navigation, including merchant shipping (except as respects inland waters, the regulation of harbours, and local health regulations); or

(8) Submarine cables; or

(9) Wireless telegraphy; or

(10) Aerial navigation; or

(11) Lighthouses, buoys, or beacons (except so far as they can consistently with any general Act of the Parliament of the United Kingdom be constructed or maintained by a local harbour authority); or

(12) Coinage; legal tender; negotiable instruments (including bank notes) except so far as negotiable instruments may be affected by the exercise of the powers of taxation given to the said parliaments; or any change in the standard of weights and measures; or

(13) Trade marks, designs, merchandise marks, copyright, or patent rights; or

(14) Any matter which by this Act is declared to be a reserved matter, so long as it remains reserved. Any law made in contravention of the limitations imposed by this section shall, so far as it contravenes those limitations, be void.

(2) The limitation on the powers of the said Parliaments to the making of laws with respect to matters exclusively relating to the portion of Ireland within their respective jurisdiction shall not be construed so as to prevent the said Parliaments by identical legislation making laws respecting matters affecting both Southern and Northern Ireland.

5. – (1) In the exercise of their powers to make laws under this Act neither the Parliament of Southern Ireland nor the Parliament of Northern Ireland shall make any law so as either directly or indirectly to establish or endow any religion, or prohibit or restrict the free exercise thereof, or give a preference, privilege, or advantage, or impose any disability or disadvantage, on account of religious belief or religious or ecclesiastical status, or make any religious belief or religious ceremony a condition of the validity of any marriage, or affect prejudicially the right of any child to attend a school receiving public money without attending the religious instruction at that school, or alter the constitution of any religious body except where the alteration is approved on behalf of the religious body by the governing body thereof, or divert from any religious denomination the fabric of cathedral churches, or, except for the purposes of roads, railways, lighting, water, or drainage works, or other works of public utility upon payment of compensation, any other property, or take any property without compensation. Any law made in contravention of the restrictions imposed by this subsection shall, so far as it contravenes those restrictions, be void.

(2) Any existing enactment by which any penalty, disadvantage or disability is imposed on account of religious belief or on a member of any religious order as such shall, as from the appointed day, cease to have effect in Ireland.

6. – (1) Neither the Parliament of Southern Ireland nor the Parliament of Northern Ireland shall have power to repeal or alter any provision of this Act (except as is specially provided by this Act), or of any Act passed by the Parliament of the United Kingdom after the appointed

day and extending to the part of Ireland within their jurisdiction, although that provision deals with a matter with respect to which the parliament have power to make laws.

(2) Where any Act of the Parliament of Southern Ireland or the Parliament of Northern Ireland deals with any matter with respect to which that Parliament has power to make laws which is dealt with by any Act of the Parliament of the United Kingdom passed after the appointed day and extending to the part of Ireland within its jurisdiction, the Act of the Parliament of Southern Ireland or the Parliament of Northern Ireland shall be read subject to the Act of the Parliament of the United Kingdom, and so far as it is repugnant to that Act, but no further, shall be void . . .

EXECUTIVE AUTHORITY.

8. – (1) The executive power in Southern Ireland and in Northern Ireland shall continue vested in His Majesty the King, and nothing in this Act shall affect the exercise of that power.

(Acts of Parliament of the UK 1920: 10 and 11 George V cap. 67.)

DOCUMENT VIII   Memorandum of General C. F. N. Macready, Commander-in-Chief of Forces in Ireland, for the Chief of the Imperial General Staff, 23 May 1921

Following the discussion we had this morning in regard to my Weekly Report, dated 14 May, I understand that you wish to be informed as to my candid opinion in regard to the *morale* and feelings of the troops at present stationed in Ireland.

It is extremely difficult for anyone not living in Ireland at the present time to realize the 'atmosphere' under which officers and men are at present serving. The rank and file are in excellent health, keen on their work, and thoroughly under discipline. During the last few months, instance after instance has occurred where officers and men have been murdered by the rebels, and yet in not one single instance has there been the least attempt at outbreak or retaliation of any kind. This, I think, speaks volumes for the state of discipline in which the troops are held by their officers. I mention that the health of the troops is good, but my Deputy-Director of Medical Services is continually impressing on me that, while this is the case at present, anything in the shape of an epidemic might suddenly have a very disastrous effect among the men who are for the most part very young and 'fine drawn'. I have on several occasions drawn attention to the number of nights in bed which in certain areas is now down to two, and this cannot be remedied except by reinforcement. While from a purely military standpoint of the well-being of the troops, the above might be considered satisfactory, I feel impelled to point out that the situation from this point of view gives me the very greatest anxiety, because there seems to be at the present moment no definite end to the state of affairs now existing. I make it my constant endeavour to keep in as close touch as may be possible with the troops, and to discover their ideas and feelings by conversations with officers of all ranks, and I believe that the following remarks are a picture of the true facts of the case: –

While the rank and file are in no way discontented, there is a feeling among them that their efforts and the danger which hourly besets them are not appreciated by people in Great Britain. The idea is strengthened by the want of anti-rebel propaganda, and by what is read in the papers about Parliamentary debates and meetings held under the auspices of very influential people. The result is that the men cannot be expected to go on indefinitely without the conditions under which they are serving having effect upon their *morale*, discipline and future from the point of view of military usefulness. Married men have been separated from their wives and families for a considerable time and see no prospect of either returning to them or having them out to live with them, and the unmarried men, except in the larger cities (and there only with increased danger) are denied the usual amusements which normally exist when serving in the British Isles.

As regards the officers, the strain upon them from the junior to the highest ranks is incomparably greater than it would be in time of actual war. The Lieutenant or Captain in charge of a village or post not only has the hourly danger of assassination hanging over him, but has to be at any moment prepared to come to a decision in regard to the defence of his charge, or to act on a sudden call from the Police, or to exercise his discretion in regard to setting right complaints which are often libellous, brought to his notice by sympathizers with rebels. In addition to this, he may be continually worried to render reports in order that questions by rebel sympathizers may be answered in the House of Commons. The strain of this situation increases in proportion to the rank of the officer concerned and in the case of General Officers Commanding Divisions, more especially in the 6th

Division whose headquarters are in Cork, it is often astonishing to me how the officers manage to bear up under the strain as they do.

Events lately have shown that the rebels stick at nothing in order to carry out their policy of endeavouring to secure their ends by outrage and murder, under the impression that the further they go, the more chance there is that the British Government and public with be cowed into submission. At the same time, it is only right to form a clear opinion of what the effect of continued service under these conditions will be upon the troops.

It is my considered opinion that the troops as at present situated will continue to do their duty during the present summer, although I am not prepared to say that, if pressed too far by the campaign of outrage directed against them, there may not be cases where they will take the law into their own hands and break out. It is difficult for the rank and file and junior officers to understand why it is that the members of Dail Eirann are left untouched by the Government, and even though Arthur Griffiths [sic] has now been under arrest for 6 months, no action is taken against him, seeing that the campaign of murder now in progress is, if not directed by the members of Dail Eirann, at all events concurred in by them. While, as I have said, I am of opinion that the troops at present in Ireland may be depended on to continue to do their best under present circumstances through this summer, I am convinced that by October, unless a peaceful solution has been reached, it will not be safe to ask the troops to continue there another winter under the conditions which obtained during the last. Not only the men for the sake of their *morale* and training should be removed out of the Irish 'atmosphere', but by that time there will be many officers who, although they may not confess it, will, in my opinion, be quite unfit to continue to serve in Ireland without a release for a very considerable period.

To sum up, it amounts to this. Unless I am entirely mistaken, the present state of affairs in Ireland, so far as regards the troops serving there, must be brought to a conclusion by October, or steps must be taken to relieve practically the whole of the troops together with the great majority of the commanders and their staffs. I am quite aware that troops do not exist to do this, but this does not alter in any way the opinion that I have formed in regard to the officers and men for whom I am responsible.

(Public Record Office CAB 24/123.)

DOCUMENT IX   Agreement between Great Britain and Irish representatives, 6 December 1921

1. Ireland shall have the same constitutional status in the Community of Nations known as the British Empire as the Dominion of Canada, the Commonwealth of Australia, the Dominion of New Zealand, and the Union of South Africa, with a Parliament having powers to make laws for the peace, order and good government of Ireland and an Executive responsible to that parliament, and shall be styled and known as the Irish Free State.

2. Subject to the provisions hereinafter set out the position of the Irish Free State in relation to the Imperial Parliament and Government and otherwise shall be that of the Dominion of Canada, and the law, practice and constitutional usage governing the relationship of the Crown or the representative of the Crown and the Imperial Parliament to the Dominion of Canada shall govern their relationship to the Irish Free State.

3. The representative of the Crown in Ireland shall be appointed in like manner as the Governor-General of Canada, and in accordance with the practice observed in the making of such appointments.

4. The oath to be taken by Members of the Parliament of the Irish Free State shall be in the following form:

> I . . . do solemnly swear true faith and allegiance to the Constitution of the Irish Free State as by law established and that I will be faithful to H.M. King George V, his heirs and successors by law in virtue of the common citizenship of Ireland with Great Britain and her adherence to and membership of the group of nations forming the British Commonwealth of Nations.

5. The Irish Free State shall assume liability for the service of the Public Debt of the United Kingdom as existing at the date hereof and towards the payment of war pensions as existing at that date in such proportion as may be fair and equitable, having regard to any just claims on the part of Ireland by way of set off or counterclaim, the amount of such sums being determined in default of agreement by the arbitration of one or more independent persons being citizens of the British Empire.

6. Until an arrangement has been made between the British and Irish Governments whereby the Irish Free State undertakes her own coastal defence, the defence by sea of Great Britain and Ireland shall be undertaken by His Majesty's Imperial Forces, but this shall not

prevent the construction or maintenance by the Government of the Irish Free State of such vessels as are necessary for the protection of the Revenue or the Fisheries.

The foregoing provisions of this article shall be reviewed at a conference of Representatives of the British and Irish Governments to be held at the expiration of five years from the date hereof with a view to the undertaking by Ireland of a share in her own coastal defence.

7. The Government of the Irish Free State shall afford to His Majesty's Imperial Forces:

(a) In time of peace such harbour and other facilities as are indicated in the Annex hereto, or such other facilities as may from time to time be agreed between the British Government and the Government of the Irish Free State; and

(b) In time of war or of strained relations with a Foreign Power such harbour and other facilities as the British Government may require for the purposes of such defence as aforesaid.

8. With a view to securing the observance of the principle of international limitation of armaments, if the Government of the Irish Free State establishes and maintains a military defence force, the establishments thereof shall not exceed in size such proportion of the military establishments maintained in Great Britain as that which the population of Ireland bears to the population of Great Britain.

9. The ports of Great Britain and the Irish Free State shall be freely open to the ships of the country on payment of the customary port and other dues.

10. The Government of the Irish Free State agrees to pay fair compensation on terms not less favourable than those accorded by the Act of 1920 to judges, officials, members of police forces, and other public servants who are discharged by it or who retire in consequence of the change of government effected in pursuance hereof.

Provided that this agreement shall not apply to members of the Auxiliary Police Force or to persons recruited in Great Britain for the Royal Irish Constabulary for the two years next preceding the date hereof. The British Government will assume responsibility for such compensation or pensions as may be payable to any of these excepted persons.

11. Until the expiration of one month from the passing of the Act of Parliament for the ratification of this instrument, the powers of the Parliament and the Government of the Irish Free State shall not be exercisable as respects Northern Ireland, and the provisions of the Government of Ireland Act, 1920, shall, so far as they relate

to Northern Ireland, remain in full force and effect, and no election shall be held for the return of members to serve in the Parliament of the Irish Free State for constituencies in Northern Ireland, unless a resolution is passed by both Houses of the Parliament of Northern Ireland in favour of the holding of such elections before the end of the said month.

12. If before the expiration of the said month, an address is presented to His Majesty by both Houses of the Parliament of Northern Ireland to that effect, the powers of the Parliament and Government of the Irish Free State shall no longer extend to Northern Ireland, and the provisions of the Government of Ireland Act, 1920 (including those relating to the Council of Ireland), shall so far as they relate to Northern Ireland, continue to be of full force and effect, and this instrument shall have effect subject to the necessary modifications.

Provided that if such an address is so presented a Commission consisting of three persons, one to be appointed by the Government of the Irish Free State, one to be appointed by the Government of Northern Ireland and one who shall be Chairman to be appointed by the British Government shall determine in accordance with the wishes of the inhabitants, so far as may be compatible with economic and geographic conditions the boundaries between Northern Ireland and the rest of Ireland, and for the purposes of the Government of Ireland Act, 1920, and of this instrument, the boundary of Northern Ireland shall be such as may be determined by such Commission.

13. For the purpose of the last foregoing Article, the powers of the Parliament of Southern Ireland under the Government of Ireland Act, 1920, to elect members of the Council of Ireland shall after the Parliament of the Irish Free State is constituted be exercised by that Parliament.

14. After the expiration of the said month, if no such address as is mentioned in Article 12 hereof is presented, the Parliament and Government of Northern Ireland shall continue to exercise as respects Northern Ireland the powers conferred on them by the Government of Ireland Act, 1920, but the Parliament and Government of the Irish Free State shall in Northern Ireland have in relation to matters in respect of which the Parliament of Northern Ireland has no power to make laws under that Act (including matters which under the said Act are within the jurisdiction of the Council of Ireland) the same powers as in the rest of Ireland subject to such provisions as may be agreed in manner thereinafter appearing.

15. At any time after the date hereof the Government of Northern

Ireland and the provisional Government of Southern Ireland here-inafter constituted may meet for the purpose of discussing the provisions subject to which the last foregoing Article is to operate in the event of no such address as is therein mentioned being presented, and those provisions may include:

(a) Safeguards with regard to patronage in Northern Ireland.

(b) Safeguards with regard to the collection of revenue in Northern Ireland.

(c) Safeguards with regard to import and export duties affecting the trade or industry of Northern Ireland.

(d) Safeguards for minorities in Northern Ireland.

(e) The settlement of the financial relations between Northern Ireland and the Irish Free State.

(f) The establishment and powers of a local militia in Northern Ireland and the relation of the Defence Forces of the Irish Free State and of Northern Ireland respectively:

and if at any such meeting provisions are agreed to, the same shall have effect as if they were included amongst the provisions subject to which the powers of the Parliament and Government of the Irish Free State are to be exercisable in Northern Ireland under Article 14 hereof.

16. Neither the Parliament of the Irish Free State nor the Parliament of Northern Ireland shall make any law so as either directly or indirectly to endow any religion or prohibit or restrict the free exercise thereof or give any preference or impose any disability on account of religious belief or religious status or affect prejudicially the right of any child to attend a school receiving public money without attending the religious instruction at the school or make any discrimination as respects State aid between schools under the management of different religious denominations or divert from any religious denomination or any educational institution any of its property except for public utility purposes and on payment of compensation.

17. By way of provisional arrangement for the administration of Southern Ireland during the interval which must elapse between the date hereof and the constitution of a Parliament and Government of the Irish Free State in accordance therewith, steps shall be taken forthwith for summoning a meeting of members of Parliament elected for constituencies in Southern Ireland since the passing of the Government of Ireland Act, 1920, and for constituting a provisional Government, and the British Government shall take the steps necessary to transfer to such provisional Government the powers and machinery requisite

for the discharge of its duties, provided that every member of such provisional Government shall have signified in writing his or her acceptance of this instrument. But this arrangement shall not continue in force beyond the expiration of twelve months from the date hereof.

18. This instrument shall be submitted forthwith by His Majesty's Government for the approval of Parliament and by the Irish signatories to a meeting summoned for the purpose of the members elected to sit in the House of Commons of Southern Ireland, and if approved shall be ratified by the necessary legislation.

(UK Acts 12 George V 1922 cap. 4, 6–11.)

DOCUMENT X   De Valera's Document no. 2, January 1922

The text omitted is the same as in the Anglo-Irish agreement, Document IX.

That inasmuch as the 'Articles of Agreement for a treaty between Great Britain and Ireland', signed in London on December 6th, 1921, do not reconcile Irish National aspirations and the Association of Ireland with the Community of Nations known as the British Commonwealth and cannot be the basis of an enduring peace between the Irish and the British peoples, DAIL EIREANN, in the name of the Sovereign Irish Nation, makes to the Government of Great Britain, to the Governments of the other States of the British Commonwealth, and to the peoples of Great Britain and of these several States, the following proposal for a Treaty of Amity and Association which, DAIL EIREANN is convinced, could be entered into by the Irish people with the sincerity of goodwill.

PROPOSED TREATY OF ASSOCIATION BETWEEN IRELAND AND THE BRITISH COMMONWEALTH.

In order to bring to an end the long and ruinous conflict between Great Britain and Ireland by a sure and lasting peace, honourable to both nations, it is agreed:-

STATUS OF IRELAND.

1. That the legislative, executive, and judicial authority of Ireland shall be derived solely from the people of Ireland.

TERMS OF ASSOCIATION.

2. That, for purposes of common concern, Ireland shall be associated with the States of the British Commonwealth, viz:
The Kingdom of Great Britain, The Dominion of Canada, the Commonwealth of Australia, the Dominion of New Zealand, and the Union of South Africa.

3. That, when acting as an associate the rights, status, and privileges of Ireland shall be in no respect less than those enjoyed by any of the component States of the British Commonwealth.

4. That the matters of 'common concern' shall include defence, peace and war, political treaties, and all matters now treated as of common concern amongst the States of the British Commonwealth, and that in these matters there shall be between Ireland and the States of the British Commonwealth 'such concerted action founded on consultation as the several governments may determine'.

5. That in virtue of this association of Ireland with the States of the British Commonwealth, citizens of Ireland in any of these States shall not be subject to any disabilities which a citizen of one of the component States of the British Commonwealth would not be subject to, and reciprocally for citizens of these States in Ireland.

6. That, for purposes of the Association, Ireland shall recognize His Britannic Majesty as head of the Association.

DEFENCE.

7. That, so far as her resources permit, Ireland shall provide for her own defence by sea, land and air, and shall repel by force any attempt by a foreign Power to violate the integrity of her soil and territorial waters, or to use them for any purpose hostile to Great Britain and the other associated States.

8. That for five years, pending the establishment of Irish coastal defence forces, or for such other period as the Governments of the two countries may later agree upon, facilities for the coastal defence of Ireland shall be given to the British Government as follows:

(a) In time of peace such harbour and other facilities as are indicated in the Annex hereto, or such other facilities as may from time to time be agreed upon between the British Government and the Government of Ireland;

(b) In time of war such harbour and other naval facilities as the British Government may reasonably require for the purposes of such defence as aforesaid . . .

. . .

10. That in order to co-operate in furthering the principle of international limitation of armaments the Government of Ireland shall not:-
(a) Build submarines . . .

MISCELLANEOUS.

12. That the ports of Great Britain and of Ireland shall be freely open to the ships of each country on payment of the customary port and other dues.

. . .

17. That this instrument shall be submitted for ratification forthwith by His Britannic Majesty's Government to the Parliament at Westminster, and by the Cabinet of Dail Eireann to a meeting of the members elected for the constituencies in Ireland set forth in the British Government of Ireland Act, 1920, and when ratifications have been exchanged shall take immediate effect.

. . .

ADDENDUM

NORTH-EAST ULSTER.

Resolved:

That, whilst refusing to admit the right of any part of Ireland to be excluded from the supreme authority of the parliament of Ireland, or that the relations between the parliament of Ireland and any subordinate Legislature in Ireland can be a matter for treaty with a government outside Ireland, nevertheless, in sincere regard for internal peace, and in order to make manifest our desire not to bring force or coercion to bear upon any substantial part of the province of Ulster, whose inhabitants may be unwilling to accept the national authority, we are prepared to grant to that portion of Ulster which is defined as Northern Ireland in the British Government of Ireland Act of 1920, privileges and safeguards not less substantial than those provided for in the Articles of Agreement for a Treaty between Great Britain and Ireland signed in London on December 6th, 1921.

(*The Times*, 5 January 1922.)

DOCUMENT XI   The Collins–Craig Pact, 30 March 1922

Heads of agreement between the Provisional Government and Government of Northern Ireland.

1. Peace is today declared.

2. From today the two Governments undertake to co-operate in every way in their power with a view to the restoration of peaceful conditions in the unsettled areas.

3. The police in Belfast to be organized in general in accordance with the following conditions:

(1) Special police in mixed districts to be composed half of Catholics and half of Protestants, special arrangements to be made where Catholics or Protestants are living in other districts. All specials not required for this force to be withdrawn to their homes and their arms handed in.

(2) An Advisory Committee, composed of Catholics, to be set up to assist in the selection of Catholic recruits for the Special police.

(3) All police on duty, except the usual secret service, to be in uniform and officially numbered.

(4) All arms and ammunition issued to police to be deposited in barracks in charge of a military or other competent officer when the policeman is not on duty, and an official record to be kept of all arms issued, and of all ammunition issued and used.

(5) Any search for arms to be carried out by police forces composed half of Catholics and half of Protestants, the military rendering any necessary assistance.

4. A Court to be constituted for the trial without jury of persons charged with serious crime, the Court to consist of the Lord Chief Justice and one of the Lords Justices of Appeal of Northern Ireland. Any person committed for trial for a serious crime, to be tried by that Court –

(a) If he so requests; or

(b) If the Attorney-General for Northern Ireland so directs.

Serious crime should be taken to mean any offence punishable with death, penal servitude or imprisonment for a term exceeding six months.

. . .

5. A Committee to be set up in Belfast of equal numbers Catholic and Protestant with an independent Chairman, preferably Catholic and Protestant alternately in successive weeks, to hear and investigate complaints as to intimidation, outrages etc., such Committee to have

direct access to the heads of the Government. The local Press to be approached with a view to inserting only such reports of disturbances, etc., as shall have been considered and communicated by this Committee.

6. IRA activity to cease in the Six Counties, and thereupon the method of organizing the special police in the Six Counties outside Belfast shall proceed as speedily as possible upon lines similar to those agreed to for Belfast.

7. During the month immediately following the passing into law of the Bill confirming the constitution of the Free State (being the month within which the Northern Parliament is to exercise its option) and before any address in accordance with Article 12 of the Treaty is presented, there shall be a further meeting between the signatories to this agreement with a view to ascertaining:

(a) Whether means can be devised to secure the unity of Ireland.

(b) Failing this, whether agreement can be arrived at on the boundary question otherwise than by recourse to the Boundary Commission outlined in Article 12 of the Treaty.

8. The return to their homes of persons who have been expelled to be secured by the respective Governments; the advice of the Committee mentioned in Article 5 to be sought in case of difficulty.

9. In view of the social conditions consequent on the political situation in Belfast and neighbourhood, the British Government will submit to Parliament a Vote not exceeding £500,000 for the Ministry of Labour of Northern Ireland to be expended exclusively on relief work, one-third for the benefit of Roman Catholics and two-thirds for the benefit of Protestants.

The Northern signatories agree to use every effort to secure the restoration of the expelled workers, and wherever this proves impracticable at the moment owing to trade depression they will be afforded employment on the relief works referred to in this Article so far as the one-third limit will allow; Protestant ex-Service men to be given first preference in respect of the two-thirds of the said fund.

10. The two Governments shall in cases agreed upon between the signatories arrange for the release of political prisoners in prison for offences before the date hereof. No offences committed after March 31, 1922, shall be open to consideration.

11. The two Governments unite in appealing to all concerned to refrain from inflammatory speeches and to exercise restraint in the interests of peace.

(*The Times*, 31 March 1922.)

DOCUMENT XII   Proclamation of the IRA leadership at the beginning of the Irish Civil War, 28 June 1922

Fellow Citizens of the Irish Republic: The fateful hour has come. At the dictation of our hereditary enemy our rightful cause is being treacherously assailed by recreant Irishmen. The crash of arms and the boom of artillery reverberate in this supreme test of the Nation's destiny. Gallant soldiers of the Irish Republic stand vigorously firm in its defence and worthily uphold their noblest traditions. The sacred spirits of the Illustrious Dead are with us in this great struggle. 'Death before Dishonour', being an unchanging principle of our national faith as it was of theirs, still inspires us to emulate their glorious effort. We, therefore, appeal to all citizens who have withstood unflinchingly the oppression of the enemy during the past six years, to rally to the support of the republic and recognise that the resistance now being offered is but the continuance of the struggle that was suspended with the British. We especially appeal to our former comrades of the Irish Republic to return to that allegiance and thus guard the Nation's honour from the infamous stigma that her sons aided her foes in retaining a hateful domination over her. Confident of victory and of maintaining Ireland's Independence this appeal is issued by the Army Executive on behalf of the Irish Republican Army.

(Poblacht na hEireann War News, no. 2, 29 June 1922.)

DOCUMENT XIII   Extracts from the constitution of the Irish Free State, December 1922

Constitution of the Irish Free State
(Saorstát Éireann)

Article 1.

The Irish Free State (otherwise hereinafter called or sometimes called Saorstát Éireann) is a co-equal member of the Community of Nations forming the British Commonwealth of Nations.

Article 2.

All powers of government and all authority legislative, executive, and judicial in Ireland derive from the people of Ireland and the same shall be exercised in the Irish Free State through the organizations established by or under, and in accord with, this Constitution.

Article 3.

Every person, without distinction of sex, domiciled in the area of the jurisdiction of the Irish Free State at the time of the coming into operation of this Constitution who was born in Ireland or either of whose parents was born in Ireland or who has been ordinarily resident in the area of the jurisdiction of the Irish Free State for not less than seven years, is a citizen of the Irish Free State and shall within the limits of the jurisdiction of the Irish Free State enjoy the privileges and be subject to the obligations of such citizenship: Provided that any such person being a citizen of another State may elect not to accept the citizenship hereby conferred; and the conditions governing the future acquisition and termination of citizenship in the Irish Free State shall be determined by law.

Article 4.

The National language of the Irish Free State is the Irish language, but the English language shall be equally recognized as an official language. Nothing in this Article shall prevent special provisions being made by the Parliament of the Irish Free State (otherwise called and herein generally referred to as the 'Oireachtas') for districts or areas in which only one language is in general use.

Article 5.

No title of honour in respect of any services rendered in or in relation to the Irish Free State may be conferred on any citizen of the Irish Free State except with the approval or upon the advice of the Executive Council of the State.

Article 6.

The liberty of the person is inviolable, and no person shall be deprived of his liberty except in accordance with law. Upon complaint made by or on behalf of any person that he is being unlawfully detained, the High Court and any and every judge thereof shall forthwith enquire into the same and may make an order requiring the person in whose custody such person shall be detained to produce the body of the person so detained before such Court or judge without delay and to certify in writing as to the cause of the detention and such Court or judge shall thereupon order the release of such person unless satisfied that he is being detained in accordance with the law:

Provided, however, that nothing in this Article contained shall be invoked to prohibit, control or interfere with any act of the military forces of the Irish Free State during the existence of a state of war or armed rebellion.

Article 7.

The dwelling of each citizen is inviolable and shall not be forcibly entered except in accordance with law.

Article 8.

Freedom of conscience and the free profession and practice of religion are, subject to public order and morality, guaranteed to every citizen, and no law may be made either directly or indirectly to endow any religion, or prohibit or restrict the free exercise thereof or give any preference, or impose any disability on account of religious belief or religious status, or affect prejudicially the right of any child to attend a school receiving public money without attending the religious instruction at the school, or make any discrimination as respects State aid between schools under the management of different religious denominations, or divert from any religious denomination or any educational institution any of its property except for the purpose of roads, railways, lighting, water or drainage works or other works of public utility, and on payment of compensation.

Article 9.

The right of free expression of opinion as well as the right to assemble peacefully and without arms, and to form associations or unions is guaranteed for purposes not opposed to public morality. Laws regulating the manner in which the right of forming associations and the right of free assembly may be exercised shall contain no political, religious or class distinction.

Article 10.

All citizens of the Irish Free State have the right to free elementary education.

. . .

Article 12.

A Legislature is hereby created to be known as the Oireachtas. It shall consist of the King and two Houses, the Chamber of Deputies (otherwise called and herein generally referred to as 'Dáil Éireann') and the Senate (otherwise called and herein generally referred to as 'Seanad Éireann'). The sole and exclusive power of making laws for the peace, order and good government of the Irish Free State is vested in the Oireachtas.

. . .

Article 14.

All citizens of the Irish Free State without distinction of sex, who have reached the age of twenty-one years and who comply with the provisions of the prevailing electoral laws, shall have the right to vote for members of Dáil Éireann, and to take part in the Referendum and Initiative. All citizens of the Irish Free State without distinction of sex who have reached the age of thirty years and who comply with the provisions of the prevailing electoral laws, shall have the right to vote for members of Seanad Éireann. No voter may exercise more than one vote at an election to either House and the voting shall be by secret ballot. The mode and place of exercising this right shall be determined by law.

. . .

Article 17.

The oath to be taken by members of the Oireachtas shall be in the following form:

I . . . do solemnly swear true faith and allegiance to the Constitution of the Irish Free State as by law established, and that I will be faithful to H.M. King George V, his heirs and successors by law in virtue of the common citizenship of Ireland with Great Britain and her adherence to and membership of the group of nations forming the British Commonwealth of Nations.

Such oath shall be taken and subscribed by every member of the Oireachtas before taking his seat therein before the Representative of the Crown or some person authorized by him.

(UK Acts 12 and 13 George V 1922 Cap. 1.)

DOCUMENT XIV De Valera's statement on the end of the Irish Civil War

Soldiers of Liberty! Legion of the Rearguard! The Republic can no longer be defended successfully by your arms. Further sacrifice of life would now be in vain, and continuance of the struggle in arms unwise in the National interest.

Military victory must be allowed to rest for the moment with those who have destroyed the Republic. Other means must be sought to safeguard the nation's right.

Do not let sorrow overwhelm you. Your efforts and the sacrifices of your dead comrades in this forlorn hope will surely bear fruit. You have saved the Nation's honour, preserved the sacred national tradition, and kept open the road of independence.

Seven years of intense effort have exhausted our people. Their sacrifices and their sorrows have been many.

If they have turned away and not given you the active support which alone could bring you victory in this last year, it is because they are weary and need a rest. Give them a little time and you will see them recover and rally again to the standard. They will then quickly discover who have been selfless and who selfish, who have spoken truth and who falsehood. When they are ready, you will be, and your place will be again as of old with the vanguard.

The sufferings which you must now face unarmed you will bear in a manner worthy of men who were ready to give their lives for their cause. The thought that you have still to suffer for your devotion will lighten your present sorrow and what you endure will keep you in communion with your dead comrades who gave their lives, and all these lives promised, for Ireland.

May God guard every one of you and give to our country in all times of need sons who will love her as dearly and devotedly as you.

(Irish Independent, 23 April 1923.)

DOCUMENT XV Constitution of Ireland, 1937 (extracts)

BUNREACHT NA HÉIREANN.

In the Name of the Most Holy Trinity, from Whom is all authority and to Whom, at our final end, all actions both of men and States must be referred,

We, the people of Éire,

Humbly acknowledging all our obligations to our Divine Lord, Jesus Christ, Who sustained our fathers through centuries of trial,

Gratefully remembering their heroic and unremitting struggle to regain the rightful independence of our Nation,

And seeking to promote the common good, with due observance of Prudence, Justice and Charity, so that the dignity and freedom of the individual may be assured, true social order attained, the unity of our country restored, and concord established with other nations,

Do hereby adopt, enact, and give ourselves this Constitution.

The Nation.

Article 1.

The Irish nation hereby affirms its inalienable, indefeasible, and sovereign right to choose its own form of Government, to determine its relations with other nations, and to develop its life, political, economic and cultural, in accordance with its own genius and traditions.

Article 2.

The national territory consists of the whole island of Ireland, its islands and the territorial seas.

Article 3.

Pending the re-integration of the national territory, and without prejudice to the right of the Parliament and Government established by this Constitution to exercise jurisdiction over the whole of that territory, the laws enacted by that parliament shall have the like area and extent of applications as the laws of Saorstát Éireann and the like extra-territorial effect.

The State.

Article 4.

The name of the state is Éire, or in the English language, Ireland.

Article 5.

Ireland is a sovereign, independent, democratic state.

Article 6.

1. All powers of government, legislative, executive and judicial, derive, under God, from the people, whose right it is to designate the rulers of

the State and, in final appeal, to decide all questions of national policy, according to the requirements of the common good.

2. These powers of government are exercisable only by or on the authority of the organs of State established by this Constitution.

Article 7.

The national flag is the tricolour of green, white and orange.

Article 8.

1. The Irish language as the national language is the first official language.

2. The English language is recognised as a second official language.

3. Provision may, however, be made by law for the exclusive use of either of the said languages for any one or more official purposes, either throughout the State or in any part thereof.

Article 9.

1. 1. On the coming into operation of this Constitution any person who was a citizen of Saorstát Éireann immediately before the coming into operation of this Constitution shall become and be a citizen of Ireland.

2. The future acquisition and loss of Irish nationality and citizenship shall be determined in accordance with law.

3. No person may be excluded from Irish nationality and citizenship by reason of the sex of such person.

2. Fidelity to the nation and loyalty to the State are fundamental political duties of all citizens.

. . .

Article 41.

. . .

3. 1. The State pledges itself to guard with special care the institution of Marriage, on which the Family is founded, and to protect it against attack.

2. No law shall be enacted providing for the grant of a dissolution of marriage.

3. No person whose marriage has been dissolved under the civil law of any other State but is a subsisting valid marriage under the law for the time being in force within the jurisdiction of the Government and Parliament established by this Constitution shall be capable of

contracting a valid marriage within the jurisdiction during the lifetime
of the other party to the marriage so dissolved . . .

. . .

Article 44.

1.   1. The State acknowledges that the homage of public worship is
due to Almighty God. It shall hold His Name in reverence, and shall
respect and honour religion.

2. The State recognises the special position of the Holy Catholic
Apostolic and Roman Church as the guardian of the Faith professed
by the great majority of its citizens.

3. The State also recognises the Church of Ireland, the Presbyterian
Church in Ireland, the Methodist Church in Ireland, the Religious
Society of Friends in Ireland, as well as the Jewish Congregations and
the other religious denominations existing in Ireland at the date of the
coming into operation of this Constitution.

(Dublin, Stationery Office, 1937.)

DOCUMENT XVI   IRA Ultimatum to the British Government, 12 January 1939

To His Excellency The Rt. Hon. Viscount Halifax, GCB

Your Excellency,

I have the honour to inform you that the Government of the Irish
Republic, having as its first duty towards the people the establishment
and maintenance of peace and order here, demand the withdrawal of
all British armed forces stationed in Ireland.

These forces are an active incitement to turmoil and civil strife, not
only in being the symbol of hostile occupation, but in their effect of
potentialities as an invading army.

It is secondly the duty of the Government to establish relations of
friendship between the Irish and all other peoples and to achieve this
we must insist on the withdrawal of British troops from our country
and a declaration from your Government renouncing all claims to
interfere in our domestic policy.

The Irish people have no cause of hostility to any European nation,
even those nations whose natural development may bring them into
conflict with British interests, and we are desirous of making it clear
that we shall in no event take part in a war of aggression against any

people or permit the nation to be regarded as having any community or identity of interest with Britain that would make us liable to attack by British enemies.

The occupation of our territory by troops of another nation and the persistent subvention here of activities directly against the expressed national will and in the interests of a foreign power, prevent the expansion and development of our institutions in consonance with our social needs and purposes – and must cease.

Neither the Government of the Irish Republic nor the Irish people are actuated by feelings of hostility to the people of Britain, rather would we welcome a better understanding but this can be brought about only on the basis that each of the two peoples is absolutely free to pursue its own course unhampered by the other. We shall regret it if this fundamental feeling is ignored and we are compelled to intervene actively in the military and commercial life of your country as your Government is now intervening in ours.

The Government of the Irish Republic believe that a period of four days is sufficient for your Government to signify its intention in the matter of the military evacuation and for the issue of your Declaration of Abdication in respect of our country. Our Government reserve the right of appropriate action without further notice if on the expiration of the period of grace, these conditions remain unfulfilled.

On Behalf of the Government and Army Council of Oglaigh na hÉireann (Irish Republican Army).

(*Wolfe Tone Weekly*, 4 February 1939.)

DOCUMENT XVII   Offer of the British Government on Irish unity, signed by Neville Chamberlain and passed to de Valera, 28 June 1940

i. A declaration to be made by the United Kingdom Government forthwith accepting the principle of a United Ireland. This declaration would take the form of a solemn undertaking that the Union is to become at an early date an accomplished fact from which there shall be no turning back.

ii. A joint Body, including representatives of the Government of Éire and the Government of Northern Ireland, to be set up at once to work out the constitutional and other practical details of the Union of Ireland. The United Kingdom Government to give such assistance towards the work of this Body as might be desired, the purpose of the work being to establish at as early a date as possible the whole machinery of government of the Union.

iii. A joint Defence Council representative of Éire and Northern Ireland to be set up immediately.

iv. The Government of Éire to invite British naval vessels to have the use of ports in Éire, and British troops and aeroplanes to cooperate with the Éire Forces and to be stationed in such positions in Éire as may be agreed between the two Governments, for the purpose of increasing the security of Éire against the fate which has overcome neutral Norway, Denmark, Holland, Belgium and Luxemburg.

v. The Government of Éire to intern all German and Italian aliens in the country and to take any further steps necessary to suppress Fifth Column activities.

vi. The United Kingdom Government to provide military equipment at once to the Government of Éire in accordance with the particulars given in the annex.

(Public Record Office PREM 3/131/2.)

DOCUMENT XVIII   Memorandum for Prime Minister (Clement Attlee) for use during debate on the Ireland Bill, 1949

Ireland Bill – Partition Question.

1. In the discussions following on the Éire Government's decision to repeal the Executive Authority (External Relations) Act the Éire Government representatives claimed to be moved by the friendliest feelings towards the United Kingdom. But the agreement that Éire should not be regarded as a foreign country was followed by an intensified campaign against partition. The campaign is supported not only by Éire Ministers but also by Mr de Valera and other Éire politicians outside the Government.

2. The main points made by Éire spokesmen are:

(i) Partition is the last bar to the establishment of friendly relations with Great Britain;

(ii) The Irish Republic cannot join the Atlantic Treaty until partition is ended because only a united country could effectively shoulder the Treaty obligations;

(iii) Ireland is essentially a single country: it is defined by the seas that surround it and its population is homogeneous, apart from religious differences;

(iv) even if it were admitted that the Northern minority had a right to form a separate state, that state ought not to include such areas as Tyrone, Fermanagh, South Down and Derry City where there are said to be Nationalist majorities;

(v) the Northern Ireland Parliament and Government do not truly represent the people of Northern Ireland and the Government are kept in power by British troops;

(vi) it has sometimes been stated that if partition were ended the Irish Republic would be prepared to leave with the Northern Ireland Parliament and Government their existing powers and would seek to exercise from Dublin only those powers which are now exercised by the United Kingdom Government.

3. Since the publication of the Ireland Bill Éire Ministers and Mr de Valera have criticised Clause 1 (1) (b) and in the proceedings on the Bill it will no doubt be attacked. Special attention will be directed to the provision declaring that 'in no event will Northern Ireland *or any part thereof* cease to be part of H.M. dominions and of the United Kingdom without the consent of the Parliament of Northern Ireland'.

4. Ministers will no doubt wish to decide in the light of what is said in the debates how far they should enter into argument about partition. The following points should be kept in mind:

(a) The opponents of partition argue as though what happened in the 1920s and 1930s was the breakaway of Northern Ireland from a united Ireland. But what really has happened is a breakaway of Southern Ireland from the United Kingdom.

(b) There is nothing inherently right in a country's being bounded on all sides by the sea. In debates on the Government of Ireland Act, 1920, (Hansard of 22nd December, 1919, column 1172) Mr Lloyd George quoted a statement by an Irish Catholic priest to the effect that the claim for a united Ireland was not likely to appeal to Europe, where Norway and Sweden and Spain and Portugal were examples of geographical boundaries not coinciding with national characteristics. Reference might also be made to Belgium and Holland, where countries which separated politically in the 19th century have now come nearer together in economic co-operation.

(c) There are undoubtedly strong divergencies between Northern and Southern Ireland and these extend through all classes. It is wholly misleading to imply that the desire to remain part of the United Kingdom is confined to a small minority in Northern Ireland.

(d) It is ludicrous to suggest that if the anti-partitionists had their way and Northern Ireland were made part of the Irish Republic, there would be a United Ireland which would shoulder the Atlantic Treaty obligations more effectively. There would be no real unity with a large minority which would feel that it had been coerced and betrayed.

(e) It seems clear that Northern Ireland business interests would be prejudiced by entering the Southern Irish economy and the Northern Ireland working man would experience a drop in his standard of living.

(f) There are admittedly strong Nationalist elements in Tyrone, Fermanagh and Londonderry. But it is impossible to draw national boundaries without including some minorities.

(University College, Oxford, Attlee Papers)

DOCUMENT XIX   Speech of Herbert Morrison, Leader of the House, in the House of Commons on the status of Northern Ireland, 11 May 1949

It is, of course, the case that Ireland, geographically . . . is very very near to our shores and we cannot be indifferent to the circumstances which obtain there. I think it is the case that if Ireland had been situated close to some other great Powers and countries in the world, the change would not have come about as smoothly as it has done, and that is very fortunate for Ireland. The country had taken this quietly . . .

Quite frankly, this Government is not going to seek and take the initiative for the purpose of losing a part of the United Kingdom . . . If Irishmen get together and make agreements among themselves that is a situation which we will consider, but it is no part of the business of this Government – and it is not going to do it – to take the initiative to diminish the territory of the United Kingdom . . .

. . . without this Bill the Republic of Ireland would be a foreign State, with all the consequences that that involves, both there and to Irish folk in this country. That is another reason why we want to get the Bill through in order to remedy that state of affairs. It was, therefore, a Commonwealth issue, and it was right that the Dominions should be consulted. But with respect to Northern Ireland, I would impress upon my hon. Friend that that is essentially a United Kingdom matter. Northern Ireland is part of the United Kingdom. Therefore, that is the domestic business of the United Kingdom Government and the Government of Northern Ireland . . .

. . . if it be the case that the British Parliament is going to declare that what was known as Éire becomes the Irish Republic and has ceased to be part of His Majesty's Dominions, surely it is logical and rational that we should in the same subsection declare what is the position regarding Northern Ireland. It is ungenerous – if I may say so, it is somewhat intolerant and unreasonable – that we should be criticized for declaring what is the position of Northern Ireland when we have been exceedingly generous in declaring the position of our country to the Republic of Ireland. Therefore, having declared the Republic of Ireland not to be part of His Majesty's Dominions, we declare that

Northern Ireland remains part of His Majesty's dominions and of the United Kingdom and affirm that in no event will Northern Ireland or any part thereof cease to be part of His Majesty's dominions and of the United Kingdom without the consent of the Parliament of Northern Ireland.

That is not banging doors but it is not unlocking doors either. It is leaving the situation fluid if the Parliament of Northern Ireland should wish to make a change, but if it does not wish to make a change, then we are affirming that the present position remains of Northern Ireland being part of the United Kingdom and part of His Majesty's Dominions and part of the British Commonwealth . . .

It must be remembered that at the moment legally the Republic of Ireland is a foreign State, and Irish folk in this country are foreigners. Indeed, the Republic of Ireland does not want to be in the Commonwealth but it does not want to be foreign – it is as far as I know quite sincere on both points. (Laughter.)

(House of Commons Debates, vol. 464, cols. 1957–65. Parliamentary copyright)

Bibliography

Students of modern Irish history are well served by a number of works, both monographs and general surveys, written in the last thirty years. This bibliography offers a selection, and is subdivided to match the chapters of the text.

The following documentary collections are recommended: A. O'Day and J. Stevenson (eds.), *Irish Historical Documents since 1800* (Savage, Maryland, Barnes and Noble, 1992); A. Mitchell and P. O'Snodaigh (eds.), *Irish Political Documents 1916–1949* (Dublin, Irish Academic Press, 1985); and A. C. Hepburn, *The Conflict of Nationality in Modern Ireland* (London, Edward Arnold, 1980). A useful work of reference is D. J. Hickey and J. E. Doherty, *A Dictionary of Irish History, 1800–1980* (Dublin, Gill and Macmillan, 1980). The journal *Irish Historical Studies* should be consulted for the latest research.

The role of myth in Irish history and the revisionist controversy are discussed in C. Brady (ed.), *Interpreting Irish History* (Dublin, Irish Academic Press, 1992); S. Richards, 'Polemics on the Irish past: the "return to the source" in Irish literary revivals', *History Workshop Journal* (Spring 1991); and R. Fanning, 'The meaning of revisionism', and D. Fennell, 'Against Revisionism', *Irish Review*, 4 (Spring 1988).

There are a number of fine syntheses. J. O'B. Ranelagh, *A Short History of Ireland* (Cambridge, Cambridge University Press, 1983), is an invigorating gallop through Ireland from prehistoric times to the modern 'Troubles'. D. G. Boyce, *The Irish Question in British Politics* (London and Basingstoke, Macmillan, 1988), is a brief paperback study of the central issues covered in this book. C. O'Halloran, *Partition and the Limits of Irish Nationalism* (Atlantic Highlands, Humanities Press International, 1987), is a stimulating survey of the main issues. More substantial are R. F. Foster, *Modern Ireland, 1600–1972* (London, Allen Lane The Penguin Press, 1988), and J. J. Lee, *Ireland 1912–1985: Politics and Society* (Cambridge,

Cambridge University Press, 1990), an iconoclastic *tour de force*. Lee's *The Modernization of Irish Society, 1848–1918* (Dublin, Gill and Macmillan, 1973), is also a stimulating read. A. T. Q. Stewart, *The Irish Question* (London, Edward Arnold, 1986), is a short account by a Unionist historian, but none the worse for that. K. T. Hoppen, *Ireland since 1800: Conflict and Conformity* (London, Longmans, 1989), is a splendid analysis of the politics of Ireland. The rather older F. S. L. Lyons, *Ireland since the Famine* (London, Collins, 1971; revised edn., 1973) has lost none of its value. His *Culture and Anarchy in Ireland, 1838–1939* (Oxford, Clarendon Press, 1979) is essential reading for its brilliant linking of cultural and political developments. The same is true of O. MacDonagh *et al.* (eds.), *Irish Culture and Nationalism, 1750–1950* (London, Macmillan, 1983). G. Dangerfield, *The Damnable Question: A Study in Anglo-Irish Relations* (London, Constable, 1977) is still worth reading as an introduction to the whole question. R. Kee, *The Green Flag* (3 vols., London, Quartet Books, 1976) is old-fashioned in approach but readable.

Economic aspects are covered in L. M. Cullen, *The Economic History of Ireland since 1660* (London, Batsford, 1972); J. M. Goldstrom and L. A. Clarkson (eds.), *Irish Population, Economy and Society: Essays in honour of the late K. H. Connell* (Oxford, Clarendon Press, 1981); C. O'Grada, *Ireland before and after the Famine: Explorations in Economic History, 1800–1925* (Manchester, Manchester University Press, 1988); M. E. Daly, *Dublin, the Deposed Capital: A Social and Economic History, 1860–1914* (Cork, Cork University Press, 1985); and P. J. Drudy (ed.), *Ireland: Land, Politics and People* (Cambridge, Cambridge University Press, 1982).

The revival of Irish nationalism in the later nineteenth century is the subject of S. Cronin, *Irish Nationalism: A History of its Roots and Ideology* (Dublin, Academy Press, 1980); O. MacDonagh, *States of Mind: A Study in Anglo-Irish Conflict, 1780–1980* (London, Allen and Unwin, 1983); D. G. Boyce, *Nationalism in Ireland* (London, Croom Helm, 1982); and T. Garvin, *The Evolution of Irish Nationalist Politics* (Dublin, Gill and Macmillan, 1981) and *Nationalist Revolution in Ireland, 1858–1928* (Oxford, Oxford University Press, 1987). D. G. Boyce (ed.), *The Revolution in Ireland, 1879–1923* (London and Basingstoke, Macmillan, 1988), contains immensely valuable material. A more specialist study is L. O'Broin, *Revolutionary Underground: The Story of the Irish Republican Brotherhood, 1858–1924* (Dublin, Gill and Macmillan, 1976). J. Sheehy, *The Rediscovery of Ireland's Past: The Celtic Revival, 1830–1930* (London, Thames and Hudson, 1980) and

J. Hutchinson, *The Dynamics of Cultural Nationalism. The Gaelic Revival and the Creation of the Irish National State* (London, Allen and Unwin, 1987), study the rise of the Irish Ireland movement. Links between literature and nationalism are also explored in D. Cairns and S. Richards, *Writing Ireland: Colonialism, Nationalism and Culture* (Manchester, Manchester University Press, 1988).

For the role of the land question in Irish nationalism and the career of Charles Stewart Parnell, the following are recommended: T. W. Moody, *Davitt and the Irish Revolution, 1846–82* (Oxford, Oxford University Press, 1982); M. J. Winstanley, *Ireland and the Land Question, 1800–1922* (London, Methuen, 1984); S. Clark and J. S. Donnelly (eds.), *Irish Peasants: Violence and Political Unrest, 1780–1914* (Manchester, Manchester University Press, 1983); W. E. Vaughan, *Landlords and Tenants in Ireland, 1884–1904* (Dublin, Economic and Social History Soc. of Ireland, 1984); R. F. Foster, *Charles Stewart Parnell: The Man and His Family* (Hassocks, Harvester Press, 1976); D. G. Boyce and A. O'Day (eds.), *Parnell in Perspective* (London, Routledge, 1991); and P. Bew, *Charles Stewart Parnell* (Dublin, Gill and Macmillan, 1980). W. M. Murphy, *The Parnell Myth and Irish Politics, 1891–1956* (New York, Lang, 1987), analyses the posthumous impact of the Parnell myth. M. Hunt and A. O'Day (eds.), *The Speeches of C. S. Parnell* (London, Hambledon Press, 1992), helps to explain the appeal of 'the uncrowned king of Ireland'. A. O'Day (ed.), *Charles Stewart Parnell: A Bibliography* (Horsham, Biblius Publishers for Meckler, 1992), surveys the substantial literature on the lost leader.

Physical-force nationalism is analysed in P. Alter, 'Traditions of violence in the Irish national movement', in W. J. Mommsen and G. Hirschfield (eds.), *Social Protest, Violence and Terror in Nineteenth- and Twentieth-Century Europe* (London, Macmillan and Berg, 1982); C. H. E. Philpin, *Nationalism and Popular Protest in Ireland* (Cambridge, Cambridge University Press, 1987); C. Townshend, *Political Violence in Ireland* (Oxford, Clarendon Press, 1983); T. P. Coogan, *The I.R.A.* (Glasgow, Fontana, 1971); and J. B. Bell, *The Secret Army: The I.R.A., 1916–79* (Swords, Poolbeg, 1989).

The changing role of the Irish question in British politics before the First World War can be followed in M. Pugh, *The Making of Modern British Politics, 1867–1939* (Oxford, Oxford University Press, 1982); G. L. Bernstein, *Liberalism and Liberal Politics in Edwardian England* (Boston, Allen and Unwin, 1986); and M. J. Winstanley, *Gladstone and the Liberal Party* (London, Routledge, 1990). *Ireland after the*

Union (Oxford, Oxford University Press, 1989), a collection of papers edited by Lord Blake, contains stimulating new material. R. F. Foster, *Lord Randolph Churchill: A Political Life* (Oxford, Clarendon Press, 1981), is very useful for the reaction of the Conservative Party to the Irish question. J. Loughlin, *Gladstone, Home Rule and the Ulster Question, 1882–93* (Atlantic Highlands, Humanities Press International, 1987); G. Morton, *Home Rule and the Irish Question* (London, Longman, 1980); F. S. Lyons, *The Irish Parliamentary Party, 1890–1910* (London, Faber, 1951); P. Jalland, *The Liberals and Ireland: The Ulster Question in British Politics to 1914* (Brighton, Harvester Press, 1980); A. Jackson, *The Ulster Party: Irish Unionists in the House of Commons, 1884–1911* (Oxford, Oxford University Press, 1989), deal with aspects of the question in greater detail. I. F. W. Beckett (ed.), *The Army and the Curragh Incident, 1914* (London, Army Records Soc., 1986), studies the crisis produced by the Curragh 'mutiny'. E. O'Halpin, *The Decline of the Union: British Government in Ireland, 1892–1920* (Dublin, Gill and Macmillan, 1987), is an account of the last phase of British government in Ireland.

For analyses of the impact of the Easter Rising, the following works are recommended: W. I. Thompson, *The Imagination of an Insurrection: Dublin, Easter 1916* (Oxford, Oxford University Press, 1967); F. X. Martin (ed.), *Leaders and Men of the Easter Rising: Dublin, 1916* (London, Methuen, 1967); A. J. Ward, *The Easter Rising* (Arlington Heights, Illinois, Davidson, Harlan Inc., 1980); U. O'Connor, *The Troubles: The Struggle for Irish Freedom, 1912–22* (London, Mandarin, 1989); and M. Ni Dhonnahadha and T. Dorgan (eds.), *Revising the Rising* (Londonderry, Fieldday, 1991) (especially the essay by J. J. Lee, 'In search of Patrick Pearse'). The best biography of Pearse is R. Dudley Edwards, *Patrick Pearse: The Triumph of Failure* (London, Gollancz, 1977). On another leader of the rising who tried to reconcile nationalism and socialism, see S. Levenson, *James Connolly* (London, Martin Brian and O'Keefe, 1973); A. Morgan, *James Connolly: A Political Biography* (Manchester, Manchester University Press, 1989); and P. B. Ellis (ed.), *James Connolly: Selected Writings* (New York and London, Monthly Review Press, 1973). Biographies of other prominent figures are B. Inglis, *Roger Casement* (London, Hodder and Stoughton, 1973), and T. P. Coogan, *Michael Collins* (London, Arrow Books, 1991).

For the Irish question in British politics after the Easter Rising and the genesis of partition, see K. O. Morgan, *David Lloyd George* (Cardiff, University of Wales Press, 1981) and *Consensus and Disunity:*

The Lloyd George Coalition Government, 1918–22 (Oxford, Clarendon Press, 1979); B. Gilbert, *David Lloyd George: A Political Life* (London, Batsford, 1987); and C. Wrigley, *Lloyd George* (Oxford, Blackwell, 1992). The 'war of independence' is analysed in S. Lawlor, *Britain and Ireland, 1914–23* (Dublin, Gill and Macmillan, 1983); C. Townshend, *The British Campaign in Ireland, 1919–21: The Development of Political and Military Policies* (Oxford, Oxford University Press, 1975), and J. McColgan, *British Policy and the Irish Administration, 1920–2* (London, Allen and Unwin, 1983). The Irish Civil War is examined in M. Hopkinson, *Green against Green: The Irish Civil War* (Dublin, Gill and Macmillan, 1988), and C. Younger, *Ireland's Civil War* (Glasgow, Fontana, rev. edn. 1979).

As a result of the opening of important archive collections in the last twenty years or so, the history of the Irish Free State/Republic can now be studied in a number of impressive works. J. A. Murphy, *Ireland in the Twentieth Century* (Dublin, Gill and Macmillan, 1975), and T. Brown, *Ireland: A Social and Cultural History, 1922–79* (Glasgow, Fontana, 1981), are recommended. E. Rumpf and A. C. Hepburn, *Nationalism and Socialism in Twentieth-Century Ireland* (Liverpool, Liverpool University Press, 1977), is a full account of political developments in the two Irish states. There are also a number of balanced studies of Éamon de Valera, including O. Dudley Edwards, *Éamon de Valera* (Cardiff, GPC Books, 1987); J. A. Murphy, and J. P. O'Carroll, (eds.), *De Valera and his Times* (Cork, Cork University Press, 1986); J. J. Lee and G. Ó'Tuathaigh, *The Age of De Valera* (Dublin, 1983); and J. Bowman, *De Valera and the Ulster Question, 1917–73* (Oxford, Oxford University Press, 1989). K. A. Kennedy, T. Giblin and D. McHugh, *The Economic Development of Ireland in the 20th Century* (London, Routledge, 1988), is a good introduction to economic aspects. Anglo-Irish relations are dealt with in D. W. Harkness, *The Restless Dominion: The Irish Free State and the British Commonwealth of Nations, 1921–31* (London, Macmillan, 1969); P. Canning, *British Policy towards Ireland, 1921–41* (Oxford, Oxford University Press, 1985); and D. MacMahon, *Republicans and Imperialists: Anglo-Irish Relations in the 1930's* (New Haven, Conn., Yale University Press, 1984). For the period of the Second World War, see B. Share, *The Emergency: Neutral Ireland, 1939–45* (Dublin, Gill and Macmillan, 1978); J. T. Carroll, *Ireland in the War Years* (Newton Abbot, David and Charles, 1975); and R. Fisk, *In Time of War: Ireland, Ulster and the Price of Neutrality, 1939–45* (London, Paladin, 1983). Some of the inanities of the unsuccessful Irish language revival campaign are well described in R. Hindley, *The Death of the Irish Language: A Qualified Obituary* (London, Routledge, 1990).

There are a number of excellent introductions to the history of Ulster Unionism and of Northern Ireland, including P. Buckland, *A History of Northern Ireland* (Dublin, Gill and Macmillan, 1981) – Buckland is also the author of a biography of the first Prime Minister of Northern Ireland, *James Craig, Lord Craigavon* (Dublin, Gill and Macmillan, 1980) – J. A. Bardon, *History of Ulster* (Belfast, Blackstaff Press, 1993); D. Harkness, *Northern Ireland since 1920* (Dublin, Helicon, 1983); S. Wichert, *Northern Ireland since 1945* (London, Longman, 1991); and A. T. Q. Stewart, *The Narrow Ground: Aspects of Ulster, 1609–1969* (London, Faber and Faber, 1977). A. T. Q. Stewart is the author of an excellent biography of the Unionist leader, *Edward Carson* (Dublin, Gill and Macmillan, 1981). M. Irvine, *Northern Ireland: Faith and Faction* (London and New York, Routledge, 1991); P. Arthur, and K. Jeffery, *Northern Ireland since 1968* (Oxford, Basil Blackwell, 1988); B. Walker, *Ulster Politics: The Formative Years, 1868–1886* (Belfast, Ulster Hist. Foundation and Inst. Irish Studies, 1989); O. Dudley Edwards, *The Sins of Our Fathers: The Roots of Conflict in Northern Ireland* (Dublin, Gill and Macmillan, 1970), are also very useful. A good brief introduction to the Unionist mentality can be found in R. G. Crawford, *Loyal to King Billy: A Portrait of the Ulster Protestants* (London, C. Hurst and Co., 1987). G. S. Walker, *The Politics of Frustration: Harry Midgley and the Failure of Labour in Northern Ireland* (Manchester, Manchester University Press, 1985), and H. Patterson, *Class Conflict and Sectarianism: The Protestant Working Class and the Belfast Labour Movement* (Belfast, Blackstaff Press, 1980), show how class and religious loyalties cut across one another in Ulster.

The literature on the modern 'Troubles' is often, and predictably, a mixture of history and journalism. Among the better examples is *Ulster* by the *Sunday Times* Insight Team (Harmondsworth, Penguin, 1972). A realistic and unemotional brief introduction is provided by *Northern Limits*, a pamphlet published in Belfast in 1992 by the Cadogan Group, a group of Northern Irish academics and others from different political backgrounds, who meet to discuss political matters. T. Wilson, *Ulster: Conflict and Consent* (Oxford, Blackwell, 1989), is a sober and realistic introduction to the problem. D. Watt, *The Constitution of Northern Ireland. Problems and Prospects* (London, Heinemann, 1981); D. Birrell and A. Murie, *Policy and Government in Northern Ireland* (Dublin, Gill and Macmillan, 1980); and M. J. Cunningham, *British Government*

Policy in Northern Ireland, 1969–1989: Its Nature and Execution (Manchester, Manchester University Press, 1991), analyse the constitutional complexities. K. Boyle, T. Haddon and P. Hilliard, *Law and State: A Case for Northern Ireland* (London, Robertson, 1975), puts the case for the continuing existence of Northern Ireland. S. Bruce, *God Save Ulster: The Religion and Politics of Paisleyism* (Oxford, Oxford University Press, 1989), is an excellent study of popular Unionism, a corrective to the idea that there are simple solutions.

Index